M

Biswadeep Ghosh studied English literature and Indian classical music before drifting towards print media. He has worked with *Outlook*, the *Hindustan Times*, *The Times of India* and Magna Publishing. Among his books are biographies of Shah Rukh Khan, Salman Khan, Aishwarya Rai and Hrithik Roshan, and two books of fiction for young adults. A freelance writer and columnist, Biswadeep is presently based in Pune.

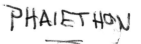
PHAIETHON

MSD

THE **MAN**, THE **LEADER**

Biswadeep Ghosh

RUPA

Published by
Rupa Publications India Pvt. Ltd 2015
7/16, Ansari Road, Daryaganj
New Delhi 110002

Sales centres:
Allahabad Bengaluru Chennai
Hyderabad Jaipur Kathmandu
Kolkata Mumbai

ISBN: 978-81-291-3581-0

Second impression 2015

10 9 8 7 6 5 4 3 2

The moral right of the author have been asserted.

Printed at Thomson Press India Ltd, Faridabad

For my uncle Dr Biplab Das Gupta,
the best parent I could have ever asked for.

CONTENTS

INTRODUCTION

HE WAS JUST an ordinary kid in Ranchi which, in the late 1990s, was a part of the state of Bihar. Like many other boys of his age, he went to school, got back home, had his lunch and rushed to MECON stadium nearby. He loved every form of outdoor sport but had been groomed to become the wicketkeeper-batsman of his school team. Soft-spoken, shy, serious about studies—though sports was what he lived for—he was called Mahi by his friends and neighbours.

Numerous success stories have demolished the clichéd conviction that morning shows the day. But, few can match the unusually obscure circumstances in which Mahendra Singh Dhoni grew up—fighting and winning over those situations make him a megastar without a counterpart in the history of Indian cricket. Observers who had seen him playing during his schooldays say that the first glimpse of his talent and temperament was seen in the inter-school finals in 1997 between DAV Jawahar Vidya Mandir (Dhoni's school) and Kendriya Vidyalaya from Hinoo, a locality in the city.

A promising wicketkeeper–batsman, who batted down the order, the then-sixteen-year-old Dhoni was a thin lad, who listened to his teachers and senior players without countering them. However, once out in the field with the bat, his personality underwent a transformation. Ruthlessly aggressive, he regularly sent the ball flying out of the ground with the mysterious power in his wrists and hands. On a good day, the young lad was capable of demoralizing the bowlers to surrender.

Before the match began, Dhoni's school, which is popularly known as DAV Shyamali, had a settled batting order. The team's regular openers were skipper Sanjeev Kumar and a technically-correct batsman Shabir Husain. Because of his attacking mindset, Dhoni was expected to step up the scoring rate towards the end of the innings. But he had other plans that day. After the team reached the ground, he surprised everybody by making a strange request to Keshab Ranjan Banerjee, his physical education teacher, whose contribution to Dhoni's career will be discussed later. 'Sir, I want to open the innings.' Banerjee was stumped by the young lad's strange request. For a minute or two, he didn't know how to respond.

Not at all keen to flirt with the batting order, and that too in the all-important final, Banerjee asked Dhoni not to make such an unreasonable demand before the start of the match. But Dhoni refused to budge. He wanted to open the innings. 'I had no idea what had hit him that day,' Banerjee remembers. Only half an hour was left for the match to begin and the teacher started to get angry with his usually obedient and mild-mannered student. Banerjee told Dhoni that opening the batting was not an option and also that he was expected to obey the instructions given to him instead of being so irritatingly stubborn.

Teacher–student confrontations aren't unheard of. But nobody expected Dhoni to turn into a rebel, who wouldn't take a 'no' for an answer. The quintessential good boy, who was every teacher's dream come true, was behaving like a brat, who wanted the teacher to follow his orders. Students in the dressing room got increasingly tense as Banerjee's anger intensified while Dhoni stuck to his guns.

Till date, Banerjee doesn't know why Dhoni wanted to open the innings. 'Maybe, he knew that he was destined to get a huge score or perhaps he simply wanted to go to bat early and spend more time at the crease. But if you ask me whether I actually know what had made him so adamant that day, I must confess that I have no idea,' Banerjee says, sitting comfortably in a blue tracksuit in his modest flat in Ranchi.

With the match about to begin, Banerjee took a calculated risk. Familiar with his student's ability to destroy the bowling attack he realized that he could take a chance with the young lad and allow him to open. If the gamble worked, Dhoni could score any number of runs in no time. If it backfired, others could do the job. Taking everybody by surprise, Banerjee asked Sanjeev to take his pads off.

Disappointed, for what would turn out to be for a brief while, Sanjeev quietly followed his teacher's orders. Before Dhoni went out to open with Shabir, Banerjee, who had kept his strategy only to himself, warned the former, 'Remember that I am sending you to bat only because you insisted on it. If you get out, no other batsman will replace you in the middle.' Dhoni nodded and walked towards the 22-yard strip with his batting partner.

When the Kendriya Vidyalaya team spotted Dhoni, its players wondered why he had been sent out to open. They believed it was a move to negate their new ball attack. By then, Dhoni had already acquired the reputation for treating the quick bowlers with disdain. What followed was a carnage in which bowlers were hit through every gap in the field on both sides of the wicket. Several aerial shots were hit with such brute force that the ball fell only after travelling for several metres beyond the boundary.

Dhoni led the charge, while Shabir, who complemented him, wasn't a quiet spectator either. He enjoyed his partner's dazzling display, but didn't hesitate to attack whenever he faced the bowling. After the score went past 200 with both the openers in full flow, Sanjeev, who had been asked to let go of his normal position, started enjoying the spectacle unfolding in front of his eyes with unconcealed glee. It seemed certain that their team would win.

Dhoni did not get out. Neither did Shabir. The former blasted his way to 213 not out from 150 balls, an innings studded with twenty-six fours and six sixes. Shabir scored an unbeaten 117 from 116 balls. They shared an opening stand of 378 runs, thus ensuring that their school won the tournament with incredible ease. Banerjee recalls with a self-indulgent smile, 'After the match ended that day, we didn't believe what had happened. The two of them had batted so brilliantly that the Kendriya Vidyalaya bowlers didn't know what to do. Winning the tournament was a special moment for all of us. Our team had put up an extraordinary score, which made our victory all the more special.'

For a schoolteacher, no achievement can be bigger than his institution's triumph in an inter-school championship. After the match ended and the trophy was theirs, the DAV students began an impromptu celebration on the ground itself. Banerjee's anger at Dhoni's obstinacy a few hours ago had diminished into a nebulous memory. As the fun continued, the shy lad whose fireworks had lit up the afternoon sky, went back to being his natural self. The teacher didn't ask a single question about his impertinence before the start of the match. On a day when an important match had been won, that issue deserved to be ignored.

For Dhoni, his 213 not out was important for two reasons. One, it showed his ability to play long knocks while scoring at a very fast pace. Two, and more importantly, Banerjee had warned him that if he lost his wicket, no other batsman would replace him at the crease. That was a hollow threat, but it kept him mindful of his responsibility and over the years, the threat became the guiding mantra of Dhoni's career—a mantra that taught him the worth of preserving his wicket when he single-handedly steered his beleaguered team out of trouble.

When we see Dhoni play a match-winning knock, especially in the shorter version of the game, we can sense a certain calmness which is rarely seen in batsmen these days. Wickets might tumble at the other end. The scoring rate might slacken due to restrictive bowling. But he is absolutely unruffled. There are times when he appears to leave too much for the end. In his mind, however, he predetermines the name of that weak link in the opposition's bowling who he decides to attack, whenever he comes on to bowl. This approach can be interpreted as a strategy. Or perhaps it is his confidence. But, there is no reason to doubt that the Indian skipper has evolved his own method of dealing with situational challenges which others can only aspire to emulate with comparable consistency.

In Twenty20 matches, he is often spoken of as the best batsman in the twentieth over of an innings. The reasoning is simple. Despite the phenomenal rate of scoring that is essential for winning these matches, he generally scores in the death overs and attacks the bowlers. Best bowlers in the world dread the very thought of bowling that twentieth over, because the identity of the person doesn't matter to Dhoni. Assisted in no small measure by his reflexes, resolve and raw power, he hits boundaries and sixes at will, knowing that he has been able to prevent a collapse by protecting his wicket in the previous overs. As long as he wins matches for his team, something he frequently does, critics have to keep their hands inside their pockets instead of taking them out to point fingers at him.

In the initial stages of his career, his approach to batting was guided by his natural flamboyance. Gradually, as his stature grew and he started leading the Indian team, his style of batting became different. Aggression came naturally to him, but he managed to tame it for the team's cause. Sometimes, he succeeded and on some occasions, he failed. Hidden behind a composed exterior was the mind of a man with an acute awareness of his role. He understood that leading from the front went way beyond astute captaincy and also that he needed to perform as a batsman as well as a keeper to guide the team on its way forward.

The story of Dhoni, the keeper was different. At the outset of his international career, he was diffident behind the stumps while keeping to the bowling of quality spinners such as Anil Kumble and Harbhajan Singh. However, he learnt the craft very soon, adapted himself to the much tougher demands of international cricket and developed into a very competent—if not orthodox—keeper, who could be expected to catch batsmen off guard with his lightning-quick reflexes, which resulted in many a fascinating instances of quality batsmen being stumped by him.

Such has cricket changed over the years that Dhoni could

have made it to the Indian team as a batsman alone now. At a time when mastery over aggressive batting has become a huge need, few of his class and temperament play the game. That he is a keeper has proved to be beneficial for him though. When he started out as a Team India player, his additional skill allowed him to consolidate his place in the team. Even after he became the captain of the Indian team, the fact that he had two roles, of a wicketkeeper and a batsman, was an advantage for him.

Ever since he took charge of the Indian team, however, Dhoni has shown that his biggest strength lies in his third role—that of a captain, who has led the team to many victories. Attributing his success to a sustained spell of good luck or a series of miracles is unfair since no man can continue to flourish for years because of either. What makes him such a fine leader? The twin virtues of observation and insight. Besides, he never gets carried away by the situation Team India is in.

Even if a victory appears to be around the corner, he never forgets that cricket being a game of uncertainties can introduce a dramatic twist to the narrative and change the plot within minutes. When the team is down and out, he tries to recover lost ground, knowing that the prospects of doom can be nullified with application and resolve. For the fighter in him, the team never goes down till it actually does.

Dhoni, a belligerent batsman. Dhoni, a good keeper. Dhoni, a very successful and shrewd captain. The young man from Ranchi has been a dedicated and illustrious servant of the game. However, many would say, and appropriately so, that his contribution to cricket lies way beyond his performance as an achiever on the field. Commentator and cricket analyst Harsha Bhogle says, 'He is the poster boy for the small-town hero. He has given hope and his is an amazing story. In a sense, he is an illustration too, as much as the trendsetter, for the ability that lay in India's interiors waiting for opportunity to come its way. I believe far more than the runs he scored or the matches he won, the message he holds out for those smaller towns will, eventually, be his larger contribution.'

The man behind the development of Jharkhand's cricketing environment, which includes establishing the wonderful JSCA International Stadium Complex in Ranchi, Amitabh Choudhary, president of Jharkhand State Cricket Association, says, 'Before Dhoni, Ranchi hadn't done anything out of the ordinary in cricket. What he has done is give hope to talented youngsters from cities that don't have a great history of famous cricketers. In fact, people living in Ranchi want to know everything about the man because he is from their own city and his role in taking the game forward has been a really special one.'

Dhoni has turned into an icon for promising Indian cricketers living in small Indian towns like Akola, Ara or Muzzafarnagar. Earlier, talented cricketers from such places seldom thought beyond playing for their districts and, if lucky, for their states. But now they can afford to dream big, knowing that if they persist and have what it takes to be in the Indian team, they might find a way to get there. After all, Dhoni has done it and how! If he could do it, so can they.

No assessment can overestimate his contribution to the sport. One cursory glance at the list of major cricketers, who have played for India, reflects a certain kind of geographical elitism. Mumbai has given numerous cricketers down the years, including institutions in batsmanship such as Sunil Gavaskar and Sachin Tendulkar. Delhi has given many players, among them the rockstar of yesteryears, Virender Sehwag, who is gradually fading away from the Indian cricket scene and the modern-day star, Virat Kohli.

The same cannot be said about Kolkata, though it did give a formidable captain like Sourav Ganguly to Indian cricket. Much before Ganguly became the captain, he had turned into a God who was infallible in the eyes of his countless fans. Even after his retirement, he continues to be the subject of worship in his birthplace. However, Kolkata, unlike Ranchi, has a couple of factors going for it. Ganguly is by far the most important player to have emerged from the city; even though long ago, Kolkata had given the odd cricketer like Pankaj Roy, who is best known for partnering Vinoo Mankad in an opening stand of 413 against New Zealand in the 1954-55 series, a record that survived for fifty-two long years. Significantly, the city has produced many luminaries in areas such as academics and culture which Ranchi cannot match. So, Ganguly, while being the most popular man in Kolkata by a fair margin even today, cannot match Dhoni's popularity in his hometown.

Mahendra Singh Dhoni's story is an inspiration for those who have enormous talent, but are preoccupied with the shortcomings that are associated with birth in a family of modest means in a small city. He has proved that a handicap is an illusion that cannot block the way of those motivated by the desire to succeed at the highest level. If he has done it, there is no reason why others, who are where he used to be, cannot reach where he has.

That is the essence of his story.

That is the essence of this story.

EARLY DAYS

THE NAME RANCHI has its origins in 'Archi,' which means bamboo grove or stave, in the language of the Oraon tribe. In modern times, purani Ranchi (old Ranchi) corresponds to the site which once had the Oraon village of Archi. The Indian subcontinent has a history that goes back to the distant past, and the capital of Jharkhand is no different. In ancient times, it is said that the Oraon and the Munda tribes were the owners of the area. The Aryans knew it as Jharkhand or the 'forest territory.' It is speculated that during the glorious reign of King Ashoka that lasted between 272 and 232 BC, the area formed a part of the Magadha Empire.

In the hundreds of years thereafter, the region experienced the rule of various dynasties, periods of peace followed by those of turbulence, uprisings and revolts. However, in recent times, the area is best-known for the formation of Jharkhand, a separate state that was carved out of Bihar on 15 November 2000. Incidentally, 15 November is also the birth anniversary of Birsa Munda, the leader of the Santhal rebellion. Babulal Marandi of the Bharatiya Janata Party became the first chief minister of the state. After the formation of Jharkhand, the twenty-eighth state of modern India, Ranchi became its capital.

Before the emergence of MS Dhoni, Ranchi's contribution

to Indian sports was rarely talked about. Hardly surprising, since the city hadn't produced any sportsman who had distinguished himself by playing cricket at the international level in a nation where the game's rule has no opposition. Most prominent sportsmen from Ranchi had made a name for themselves in the field of hockey, which is officially the national sport of India, but miles behind cricket in terms of actual popularity.

Encouraged by Christian missionaries, hockey flourished in the area. The tribal population took to it passionately, the result being that some of them rose from obscurity to become significant contributors to India's story of success in the sport. Among those who came from Ranchi was Jaipal Singh Munda, who captained the Indian hockey team at the 1928 Amsterdam Olympics during the league phase. Michael Kindo played for the bronze-medal-winning Indian team at the 1972 Munich Olympics, while Sylvanus Dung Dung was part of the team that won the gold at the 1980 Moscow Olympics.

In recent times, Ranchi has produced another remarkable sportsman—a young archer named Deepika Kumari, a three-time winner of the silver medal in the World Cup finals. The daughter of an auto-rickshaw driver, and a nurse working at the Ranchi Medical College, it was only after her twin victories at the 2010 Commonwealth Games that she managed to convince her father about her talent in the sport. Hers is a significant story, yet, few sports lovers associate her name with the place she comes from.

In the city—from where Deepika and several hockey players have represented India—is a mansion in a locality called Harmu Housing Colony. The sight of people slowing down their vehicles to have a casual glance at it is hardly uncommon. Seen from the outside, the house, while huge, isn't an architect's delight. But there are all sorts of stories about it. It is said to hide a mini museum of superbikes. Some chatterboxes make every effort to convince the listener that its rooms are as big as those in Buckingham Palace. There are all kinds of conflicting descriptions of its interiors, which can be a tad entertaining on certain occasions. Those who cook up such stories are hardcore devotees of Dhoni, which is why they try every method possible to glorify their icon. If ridiculous exaggeration can be one way of expressing their pride, so be it.

Another reason why the locals respect their boy is the manner in which he managed to soar above the limitations of his ordinary background, Team India's skipper being one of the three children of Paan Singh and Devki Devi, who were tormented by financial worries before and after his birth and even after he had stepped into adulthood. An interesting story many people in Ranchi love to share is that, even after his son had started playing for India, Paan Singh used to enjoy his bicycle rides. In spite of his son's phenomenal success and the money that came with it, he didn't forget his roots, a quality that continues to be appreciated by those who had seen him enjoy the simple pleasures of life even after Dhoni had become a celebrity cricketer.

Hailing from a village named Talasaalam, which is at a distance of 15.5 miles from Almora in the state of Uttarakhand, Paan Singh knew what experiencing hardships in his native place was all about. The surroundings in which he had grown up were picturesque. Living in this environment, he struggled to find beauty and comfort in life. He married Devki Devi, a deeply religious lady from Nainital, and tried to make a living as a farmer. During those days transportation was not easily available. People had to walk for more than ten kilometres to reach a spot where buses were available. Farming wasn't profitable, and Paan Singh wasn't equipped to enjoy the benefits of good education either. He needed a job, a job of any kind, to lead an ordinary life. Somehow, he wanted to find a way out of the difficult situation he was in.

Eventually Paan Singh left Almora with his wife because he was desperate to find a job that paid well. Since he didn't have proper academic qualifications, his situation was similar to that of innumerable unemployed Indians who have to make do with whatever they get for less money. The Dhoni family first reached Lucknow where Paan Singh failed to find a suitable opportunity. So, he went to Bokaro where a steel plant was being built. That implied opportunities for employment. But after he reached there, he realized that he was late and all the recruitments had already been made.

Finally, he landed in Ranchi where he started out as an unskilled worker with Hindustan Steel Authority. Many years later, he would retire as the work supervisor with MECON Limited, an autonomous body of consultants in the field of engineering, which reports directly to the Union Government's Ministry of Steel and Mines.

The couple had three children—a son whom they named Narendra, followed by daughter Jayanti, and Mahendra, the youngest one, who was born on 7 July 1981. The kids attended DAV Jawahar Vidya Mandir in Shyamali colony where Mahendra showed glimpses of his talent in various sports such as cricket, table tennis, football and badminton.

During his struggling days, Paan Singh had been assigned to work as a pump operator to water the roads of Shyamali colony. His only personal connection with the game—if one can call it that—was when he had to take charge of the water supply on the pitch during a Ranji Trophy match between Bihar and Odisha, then known as Orissa.

As a youngster, Mahendra, who was better known as Mahi or even Mahia, lived in a small flat situated inside a narrow lane in Shyamali colony behind the MECON stadium. Narendra, his eldest brother, goes back in time to resurrect a memory of the young Mahi, 'Mahi used to go to school in the mornings and get back home by three in the afternoon. After having lunch, he used to rush to the MECON stadium since it was located close to our house.' A small stadium with nominal seating capacity, MECON stadium was nevertheless, a great place to practise and learn.

During his early days, Dhoni was a football goalkeeper. But he did find time for some cricket too. Umakant Jena, who has been the ground in-charge of the stadium for the last twenty-seven years, remembers a story from Dhoni's childhood, 'Mahi started playing in this stadium when he was very young.' 'His father was very particular about his children's studies. So he used to scold Mahi for playing a lot instead of studying. He was right, because there were times when Mahi did spend too much time in the stadium. When I noticed it, even I scolded him and asked him to go back home,' he says.

Dhoni did not top his class. But, as his father would tell *rediff.com* in 2007, 'Let me tell you that the boy was not a weak student. These days parents want their kids to get 95 or 99 per cent. He would play cricket and other stuff which made it a bit difficult. But he was a good student. He did not score the highest marks in the class. But he always got a first division. He was interested in his studies. He never got a third division. Or failed.'[1]

Distraction was not a part of his mental make-up. This made him a formidable opponent in sports and good enough in studies. Seemant Lohani studied with Dhoni from nursery till Standard XII. One of Dhoni's best friends even today, he reflects, 'He just wanted to give it his best shot in everything he did. In sports and also in studies, he followed the same principle. During his schooldays, he would write his exams. Inside a bus, the team would be waiting for him to finish his exam papers. After he was through, he would go with the team, play the match, go back home and make sure he was fully prepared for the examination scheduled for the next day.'

A young Dhoni wasn't much of a foodie. What he simply adored was milk. His father went to the cowshed personally and made sure that he got fresh milk for his son, by standing right there while the cow was being milked.[2] His elder brother Narendra adds, 'He was very fond of roti and alu ki sabzi. He used to make a roti roll with potatoes in it and have a quick meal so that he could be on the field as soon as he possibly could.'

Apart from playing, Dhoni had another love: video games. When he played video games, the world around him ceased to exist. There were times when his friends kept calling him, but he simply didn't hear them. That he is passionate about video games even today doesn't surprise Seemant, who says, 'Although Mahi has become a huge name, he hasn't changed one bit. Whenever he comes to Ranchi, he comes down to

[1]'The boy from Ranchi,' *Rediff News*. http://www.rediff.com, 16 March 2007 (accessed 15 December 2014).
[2]Ibid.

my house on an ordinary motorcycle, wearing a full helmet so that people on the streets do not recognise him. We chat and have breakfast together. Of course, he doesn't have the kind of time like he used to have before. After all, he is the captain of the Indian cricket team.'

THE BEGINNING

DHONI WOULD HAVE continued to play football if fate
hadn't intervened in the form of Keshab Ranjan Banerjee,
his sports-crazy physical education teacher at DAV Shyamali.
It was Banerjee who spotted a young Dhoni while he was
practising goalkeeping for the Shyamali Football Academy at
the MECON stadium. At that time, the school team was on
the lookout for a specialist keeper and Banerjee's experienced
eyes gauged that the young lad was a possible solution.

Suitably impressed by his reflexes, he informed Chanchal
Bhattacharya, a journalist for the local daily *Ranchi Express*
and also a qualified coach from the Netaji Subhash National
Institute of Sports, Patiala. Popularly known as Chanchalda,
Bhattacharya was the coach of the DAV East Zone team
which consisted of players selected from various branches of
DAV schools spread across the East Zone.

Dhoni was initially reluctant to make a sudden switch.
While he enjoyed cricket, his passion for football was intense.
But he was convinced to wear the keeper's gloves, and was
even made to go through intense practice sessions before being
allowed to play his first competitive match in 1994. Chanchalda
distinctly remembers, 'He played his first match as a keeper in
the Ranchi District Inter-school Cricket Tournament against

Central Academy School, Bariatu, in the MECON stadium. He only gave away four byes in a match that his school won.' So impressed was the coach that he also made him a part of Commando's XI, a local Ranchi club. 'In his school team, he batted in the middle order. But for the club, I sent him to bat at number seven or eight. Even if he scored 10, it had one six in it.'

Banerjee remembers Dhoni as a boy with 'tremendous willpower and sincerity.' 'When we had matches, there were times when he used to be inside the classroom with the bus waiting to leave for the venue. The team would wait for him. I wanted him to board the bus earlier, but he left the class and joined us only after the period got over. When I think of it today, it is this approach to life that has made him such a fine player. He was a focused boy. Besides, he was always very calm, which shows in his captaincy today.'

Everybody who knew Dhoni during that period talks about him as a quiet lad. Banerjee says, 'He hardly expressed himself verbally, while his love for sports was immense. When students become slightly senior, they have a tendency to get distracted by girls. But one cannot say any such thing about Mahi.' Sanjeev Kumar, who captained his school side, shares a different story though. 'He liked girls, especially those with short hair. But the problem with him was that he had no guts. After he grew familiar with his seniors, he would request them to introduce him to a girl he might have liked. But doing that for him was useless. He couldn't talk to any girl even for five minutes.'

Talking to girls might have been a problem, but hitting the ball out of the ground after he became a regular in the school team certainly wasn't. Having witnessed his ability to massacre the opposition's bowling from day one, Sanjeev wonders where Dhoni's power came from. 'His idea of snacking was mostly limited to golgappa and egg roll. Although he played a lot, he didn't indulge in any special exercises. He led a normal life like all of us but had amazing strength in his hands.'

After he became a part of the school's playing XI, Sanjeev noticed that the young lad had an important quality that goes into the making of any successful person—determination. He spotted it for the first time when the school's supplier of cricketing equipment delivered a consignment of bats of substandard quality. 'The wood was so bad that hitting shots with those bats was out of question.'

Everybody gave up, apart from Dhoni. 'I told Mahi several times that attempting to play a match with one of those bats was impossible. But he just didn't listen. He took his bat home, made several holes in it with a compass, and poured pickle oil in them. Even after that, the bat continued to be in a terrible shape. He kept on pouring pickle oil and working on the bat till it became good enough to play with. Eventually, Mahi transformed the piece of wood into a decent bat and actually used it in cricket matches. That is when I knew that this guy would go really far.'

Time went by. Sanjeev continued to captain the team, while Dhoni played as the keeper, who was expected to make the run rate fly towards the end of an innings. During that time, the team's management was strict and defeats were unacceptable. Chanchalda recalls, 'During those days, whenever the school lost a match, the players were not allowed to board the team bus. They walked back to school.' Under the guidance and supervision of Chanchalda, Dhoni continued to evolve as a player. However, his first brush with fame in school cricket circles was on its way.

Then came the day when Shabir and Dhoni went on to share that massive 378-run partnership which piloted their school to a win in the inter-school finals. Since Dhoni had been particularly aggressive, the news of his powerful strokeplay spread throughout Ranchi's cricketing circles. He became a much sought-after batsman in local tennis ball tournaments in which the batsmen were expected to score runs at a very fast pace. Dhoni happily obliged. He didn't follow the cricketing manual; but then, who gives a damn to rules in local tennis ball matches anyway? Gradually, he became a popular figure, who was particularly harsh on the fast bowlers and smashed them to all parts of the ground.

Ranchi has had an interesting tradition of tennis ball tournaments, where small cash prizes are offered for every six and four that the batsmen hit. Apart from more awards in cash for the winners and runners-up, Jena informs that there are tournaments which offer 'live goats and chickens to the finalists so that they can cook them and enjoy a great meal thereafter.' Such temptations were irresistible for the local players, who couldn't have asked for anything more. Hence, having a batsman like Dhoni, who could win a match in a few overs, worked best.

In modern times, if there is one shot Dhoni is identified with, it is his peculiar helicopter shot which sends the cherry soaring out of the boundary with the sheer power of his wrists and forearms. Chanchalda believes that the shot ought to be attributed to his experience in playing tennis ball cricket. He explains, 'Tennis balls are very light and have to be hit with force to reach the boundary. It is during those matches that Dhoni developed this technique which has stayed with him ever since.'

However, Dhoni has often said that the inspiration for this shot was the late Santosh Lal, who passed away after suffering from pancreatitis in July 2013. The two, who had met while representing the U–19 team, became great buddies who loved to play pranks. When Dhoni got to known about Lal's illness while holidaying in New York, he got him air-lifted to Delhi from Ranchi for further treatment. However, Lal who was renowned for playing that shot passed away, leaving a huge void in Dhoni's life.

As a young boy, Dhoni was attracted to bikes and driving. He used to zip around in Ranchi on his father's scooter, guilty of underage driving in a city where disobeying rules wasn't frowned upon. It was a passion that would culminate in his wellknown collection of bikes.

Dhoni's love for sports went well beyond cricket. He loved playing carrom and was also good at it. His goalkeeping skills had been eclipsed by his ability to play cricket, and he was passionate about badminton as well. Chanchalda shares, 'He is a good badminton player even today and has tremendous stamina and energy for the feathered sport.' Banerjee tells an interesting story about Dhoni's participation in a local tournament. 'Mahi could spare very little time for playing badminton compared to those who played the game regularly. However, he put up a very good show and actually reached the third round.'

Even today, whenever Dhoni is in Ranchi, he goes to practise badminton at the DAV auditorium. He continues to chase and hit the feathered target for three hours without a break. Banerjee once asked him what makes him take the game so seriously. Dhoni's response revealed the presence of a thinking mind. 'Sir, if I play it and a good smash comes back to me at the speed of 240 kmph which I manage to return, I can easily deal with fast deliveries that are 100 kmph slower.' The explanation didn't come from Mahi. Instead, this was 'Captain Cool' speaking.

During his younger days, nobody had a clue about the way Dhoni's mind worked when he played for the school team and Commando's XI. Soon after he had made it to the club team, he was selected to play for the Bihar team for the Vinoo Mankad U-16 Championship in Delhi in which he did quite well. Bhattacharya, who played an important role in the early part of his career, was the coach of the state U-16 team too. After playing for Commando's XI from 1995-98, Dhoni also had a stint with the (RDCIS) Research and Development for Iron and Steel team in Ranchi which paid him a stipend of ₹1100. It was while he was playing for the RDCIS that a gentleman named Deval Sahay stepped in and helped him take an important step forward.

Sahay, while working with MECON, had met Dhoni, who was then a young boy. Paan Singh, who was responsible for providing water for curing the grass at the stadium, was close to Sahay, the secretary of the Ranchi District Cricket Association during that period. In 1998, Sahay made an interesting offer to Dhoni. He asked the young lad whether he would like to play for the Central Coalfields Limited (CCL), the company he was then working for. It was an offer that Dhoni readily accepted.

Interestingly, when asked why he wanted to play for CCL, the young cricketer said that he would get more practice sessions and more matches to play which will help him improve his game. While playing for RDCIS, Dhoni batted in the lower middle order. He wanted to bat up the order and was optimistic that the new team would give him that opportunity.

Dhoni was in class XI when he joined the CCL team. He was paid a monthly stipend of ₹2200, apart from travelling allowance, daily allowance and free medical benefits. Dhoni's stipend was three hundred more than the other players. Having seen and heard about the young lad's phenomenal potential, Sahay decided that asking Dhoni to bat up the order could be well worth a gamble. Dhoni didn't disappoint him, in fact, scored five centuries in his first five innings.

Playing for CCL was a huge challenge for the young man. He had to attend his classes and also play anywhere between thirty and fifty matches in a year. Being the impeccably disciplined lad that he was, he trained hard during the nets and never ever missed his practice sessions. Sahay recalls, 'Often he would come for practice in the morning and play a match later in the day.'

Although he was the youngest player in the CCL team, Dhoni's talent earned him the love and respect of his teammates. His batting became so important for CCL that while other players were given fifteen minutes each for net practice, he was allowed to practise for half an hour. Even after his practice session was over, he persuaded bowlers to bowl at him so that he could master his defensive strokes in order to become a complete batsman, which might seem amusing to some since Dhoni is destined to be remembered by posterity for his uniquely unorthodox attacking shots.

It was while he was playing for CCL that Dhoni gradually began to attract big crowds. In small places such as Sial, Muri and Khelari, where many CCL matches were played, the grounds were packed with ordinary cricket lovers who turned up to watch him bat. Seeing his highly unusual batting technique was a temptation, but what aroused a lot of interest was his ability to bludgeon the bowling. Talking about Mahi's approach as a batsman at that time, Bhattacharya says, 'He simply didn't believe in defending, and honestly, did play too many rash strokes at times. During that period, he never ever differentiated between a good ball and a bad one.'

Everybody, right from his coaches to his seniors, remembers him as a lad who hardly spoke, and Sahay is no different. 'He was always very humble, which made him a very endearing guy.' Sanjeev, who captained Dhoni, adds, 'When we played together, I never saw any leadership quality in him. All he wanted to do was go out and score as many runs as possible. We knew he had a very special gift from heaven, but the interesting thing was that he hardly gave any suggestions to me. Today, when I see him lead the team, how I wish I had known about his hidden leadership skills as well.'

It was while he was playing with his new team that Dhoni's talent as a batsman truly blossomed. One major reason was that he was promoted to the number three spot in the batting order, which was much higher than his usual number seven. That allowed him to spend a lot more time in the middle. Longer periods of batting at the nets and spending more time at the crease in actual matches are not the same thing. Dhoni realized that even as he continued to strike the ball and score runs at the sort of pace he was identified with earlier.

Another quality of Dhoni which Sahay observed from very close quarters was that the lad, who was at his best against the quicks, was unfazed by injuries and wanted to be on the field even when he ought to have stayed away from it. The gentleman distinctly remembers the occasion when the CCL team was playing a tournament in Odisha. While batting, Dhoni was hit by a rising delivery which fractured his left hand.

Even from a distance, Sahay could see that Dhoni needed urgent medical attention. He was asked to come back, and a fracture was identified immediately. The doctor bandaged his hand, and asked Dhoni to rest. But that was not to be. Brave and somewhat reckless too, Dhoni decided to return to the field and bowled his team to victory. His injury didn't allow him to wear his keeping gloves, because of which a part-time keeper did his job. Even today, Dhoni cannot resist bowling the odd over of gentle-medium pace which is hardly effective against international opposition. But he continues to bowl, since his occasional spells during his young days had wicket-taking potential against infinitely inferior opposition.

Some residents of Shyamali colony who play cricket and football at the MECON stadium today share that one commonplace story of hitting the ball out of the small ground on countless occasions. Sahay recalls an interesting episode which took place while Dhoni was playing for CCL at the Loyola Ground in Jamshedpur in an inter-office final match against TISCO. While playing one of his long and high shots, Dhoni ended up hitting the ball so hard that it flew out of the ground and landed on the asbestos roof of the Deputy Commissioner's house situated at a distance of 200 metre from the pitch. The ball made a hole in the roof. Police guards seized the ball and subsequently rushed to the stadium to identify the guilty batsman. The organizers had to interfere and deal with the police. Eventually, the then Deputy Commissioner arrived at the spot and ordered the guards to return the ball. The big news for CCL was that it won the match as well as the tournament later.

Dhoni's story during the initial phase of his career will

remain incomplete without a mention of Paramjit Singh, the owner of a small sports shop in Ranchi's Sujata Chowk. As youngsters, Dhoni and Singh used to play gully cricket which is how their friendship developed. When Dhoni had started playing really well at the school level, Singh, who hadn't quite established his own business till then, began pursuing the Ludhiana-based manufacturers of Beat All Sports (BAS) bats, for an annual supply of free cricketing gear. Initially, the owners refused to comply with his request. But when Singh became persistent, they eventually gave up and agreed to give the young man an annual supply of bats and other necessary cricket gear. Sanjeev recollects this story, as does Banerjee and everyone else who has been associated with Dhoni's sporting life during his formative years.

In recent times, Singh prefers not to talk about Dhoni. But if one casually asks him to share the story of his contribution to the Indian captain's career, he philosophically replies, 'I have done nothing at all. God was kind to him. He was blessed with supreme talent. He would have gone where he has with or without my little assistance.'

Today, Dhoni is at the peak of his cricketing glory. He is busy, popular, deified. One person had predicted his destiny, albeit in jest, while he was still in school. Once, when he had boarded the school bus late, a girl who studied with him remarked sarcastically, 'Take his autograph now. You guys may not be able to meet him once he grows up.' Banerjee, who shares this story, doesn't remember her name. Little did the girl know that what she was saying then would prove to be partially true later.

JOURNEY TO KHARAGPUR

BY THE TIME he was in his late teens, Dhoni was already a promising cricketer, who had represented the Bihar U-19 team during the 1998-99 season in the Cooch Behar Trophy. In January 2000, he made his first-class debut for Bihar in the Ranji Trophy. However, since his batting and wicketkeeping techniques weren't orthodox, there was this one important question whose answer everybody was waiting for. How far will Mahendra Singh Dhoni go?

A former Team India cricketer, who shall remain unnamed, remembers, 'I had the opportunity to see Dhoni as a young man during his U-19 days. He was hardly well built but had the ability to hit seriously powerful strokes that astonished me. As and when he got going, he sent the ball flying out of the ground with a frequency that was plain unimaginable.'

Talking about Dhoni's keeping ability, he adds, 'From a distance, he wasn't attractive to watch. But what made him more than useful was that he would take catches and execute quick stumpings. In short, he was what one would call an effective wicketkeeper.' When he had seen Dhoni during that period, did he ever think that the boy would become what he has? 'Frankly, no. Never,' he responds, 'Even then, it was evident that he had the ability to do well at the zonal level.

At that time, however, the thought that he would go on to play for India never even came to my mind.'

Born into a lower middle class family, their financial situation compelled him to seek a job to assist them with a regular supply of money. In spite of being a Ranchi boy who had entertained the local crowds and also played for Bihar, he had failed to find regular employment in the city. By the time he was a twenty, he was desperately hunting for a job. That's when Kharagpur happened.

A sleepy town in West Bengal, Kharagpur is best known for the Indian Institute of Technology and the world's longest railway platform. Dhoni happened to know Satyaprakash Krishna, a Train Ticket Examiner (TTE, usually referred to as a ticket collector), in Kharagpur. It was Krishna who did all the paperwork so that Dhoni could apply through the sports quota and Dhoni underwent the customary rituals and got the job.

Later, the young keeper–batsman was introduced to the late Animesh Ganguly, the then Divisional Railway Manager (DRM) of South Eastern Railway (SER). A well known cricket fanatic, Ganguly was trying to find a player who could combine both the roles for the SER team.

Although he had played in the Ranji Trophy, Dhoni was made to go through a test before being selected for the SER team. The DRM went with him to the South Eastern Railway Sports Association (SERSA) Stadium and introduced him to Subrata Banerjee, who responded to his nickname, Baghada, in the local circles. A former cricketer, who had also played for the squad Dhoni was being tested for, Baghada wanted to retire from the game as he had turned forty-one by then. Ganguly, who knew about his ability to train the juniors, had asked him to take up coaching instead of saying goodbye to the game altogether.

During selection, the Ranchi boy was made to face sixty deliveries. An ordinary cricketer, who wanted to play for his employer's team, might have been circumspect and would have probably abstained from showcasing his entire repertoire of strokes, but not Dhoni. He played his natural game and hit the ball with the sort of power which he was identified with back home. After the trial was over, Dhoni became a TTE who also played for the SER team.

Krishna recalls that the twenty-year-old was given platform duty, a role in which he had to check the tickets of passengers. During his initial days in the city, he used to stay with Krishna at his residence in the Traffic colony. The house was shared by Robin Kumar, Jai Shukla and Deepak Singh, three other SER employees who also played for their organisation's cricket team. After Krishna got married in 2002, the bunch of bachelors had to move out.

When Dhoni used to relax at home with his fellow flatmates, he couldn't resist being attracted to a particular sight. 'He was very fond of watching fighter jets that took off from the Kalaikunda air base near Kharagpur. The jets flew very low and fast. Each time one of them flew over our place, he ran out to admire the aircraft. The speed and sound held him spellbound,' says Krishna, reminiscing about the past.

Watching cricket matches on the television was a must for Dhoni. However, there was one big problem that Krishna, being the eldest one, had to frequently deal with. There being just one television at home and too many channels to choose from, his younger flatmates had arguments regarding which channel to watch.

One day, Deepak was enjoying the Amitabh Bachchan starrer *Muqaddar Ka Sikandar* late at night. Another channel was showing a recorded match between India and Australia at Sharjah at the same time. Deepak wanted to see the film. Dhoni was desperate to watch the match. Both had an intense argument which led to a fight, resulting in a slight damage to the television. Krishna, who had been a spectator all along, had to intervene. He decided in favour of Dhoni and all of them watched the match together.

Apart from the occasional difference of opinion, all the flatmates bonded brilliantly because of their common passion— cricket. Among them, Robin, who hailed from Chhattisgarh, captained the SER team. Like Dhoni, he too worked as a TTE which meant that each of them spent long hours away from the flat. Robin, who cannot hide his astonishment at the size of cricketers' kits these days, remembers, 'In Kharagpur, Dhoni moved around with only one bag. He never wanted more than what was required in terms of clothes or other accessories.'

A teetotaller, Dhoni would nevertheless sit with his friends when they found time to enjoy an evening together with a few drinks. On one such occasion, a friend of his started teasing him about his dislike for alcohol. Being the sort of stubborn chap that he was, he took it up as a challenge and decided to finish a bottle of beer at one go. The moment he picked up the bottle, his friends were convinced that he would be able to polish off the contents at one go. Instead, he had two gulps after which he ran out of the room and threw up.

During his stay in Kharagpur, Dhoni shifted residences a few times. He stayed with Krishna and other friends until the former got married. He also lived in the SERSA Stadium in a room that he shared with Jai, his former flatmate in Krishna's house. Later, the young cricketer, whose first salary was a meagre ₹5,500 a month, shared a place with Robin and Jai in Golkhuli near the Traffic Area.

Although Dhoni stayed in Kharagpur for less than four years, he has left many fond memories behind. Since he was a sports quota recruit, he was officially spared from regular duty to play cricket for SER. Baghada remembers, 'He followed the principle of three Ds—Dedication, Determination and Discipline—thoroughly. Even in the off-season, when other players seldom came to the ground, Dhoni would throw a tennis ball on the wall and catch it at different angles to stay in touch with keeping. In fact, he often requested me to allow him to play with children so that he could stay in shape in the off-season as well.' He also did a lot of keeping in the Kharagpur Blues Cricket Coaching Camp run by Baghada, and played football to stay fit. 'He enjoyed being on the ground which not only helped him at that time but also proved to be immensely beneficial in the long run,' reflects the veteran coach.

As a batsman playing in the DRM Cup Tournament, an inter-departmental tournament of the SER, Dhoni had very different ideas about his role. Years after he had opened the innings and scored 213 not out for his school against Kendriya Vidyalaya in Ranchi, he would dream of playing as an opener very often. 'During his days with the SER, he always wanted to open. But he was made to play at number three or four, which disappointed him. Although he never questioned my decisions, he did voice his anguish,' says Baghada.

Currently the coach of SER and SERSA teams and posted as an Accounts Assistant in Kharagpur, Baghada has wonderful memories of Dhoni. Baghada's most vivid recollection of

Dhoni's intrepid batting is his knock in a match in which his team was playing against its counterparts from Odisha. As was the case in most matches, the tie was limited to forty overs per side. The SER team had a steep target in front of them. 'By the time Dhoni went out to bat at number three, a mountain had to be climbed and merely eleven overs were left. When he told me that he didn't have much time left, I asked him to do something for the sake of the team. In other words, just go out there and hit a century. He heard me out, went out to bat and ravaged the Odisha bowlers, who simply didn't know what had hit them. He played with exceptional courage, scored a century and won the match for us with two balls to spare,' he says.

There was another match in which Baghada saw the young boy in full flow—one that was being played so that he could select the SER team. Dhoni's participation in the match was a mere formality. However, on his part, Baghada had divided the players very carefully so that both the teams were equally balanced.

Every prominent sport has local heroes. If Dhoni was the superstar who had travelled quite far as a first-class cricketer, Dhoni's Kharagpur buddy Jai was not far behind in the local circles. A fast bowler, Jai could bowl with such furious pace that he literally put the fear of God in the opposition. Known to be brutal against pacemen, Dhoni went after him. After he came out to bat Jai bowled the first over that he faced. He was hit for 26 runs. That was just the beginning of a storm as Dhoni eventually scored 166 runs from 66 balls.

Baghada was guiding Dhoni at a very crucial stage of his career. An attractive stroke-maker, who was reliable behind the wickets and played at the domestic first-class level, the young man's talent had convinced the veteran coach that he could become a long-distance runner in the game. Way back in 2001, Baghada had observed Dhoni's single-minded devotion to the game that inspired him to perform even when the challenge in front of him wasn't that tough.

He still remembers the day when Dhoni was asked to open for his team in a thirty-five-over match at the SERSA Stadium. It was just a friendly tie, which is why everybody else in the team had enjoyed a leisurely breakfast before coming to the stadium. But not Dhoni, who simply had two slices of bread for breakfast. 'Since his team was supposed to play after lunch, he skipped the afternoon meal to make sure that he stayed light during the match. Even before the rest of the players had returned from the break, he was all padded up and ready before anyone else,' he says.

Another quality which Baghada distinctly remembers is that Dhoni never differentiated between his teammates and rivals. He played hard until the last ball was bowled. He didn't want to lose a single match. When in full flow, he carted the bowlers all over the ground. Once the match was over, however, he sat inside tea stalls and sipped hot cups of tea with his rivals. Dhoni's friendly quality sometimes irked his fellow team members, but it never quite bothered Dhoni and he refused to change his approach.

Dhoni didn't long to become a well known player in Kharagpur. Far away from home, was he happy? Initially, he wasn't. He had left his family and friends in Ranchi and come to a new city. He was part of the SER team, which allowed him to do what he liked most. But that was far from enough, and that resulted in bouts of sadness.

It was only after his introduction to tennis ball cricket that things changed for the better. Tennis ball cricket in Kharagpur was a different challenge. Also known as 'khep' cricket, it was played on 18-yard pitches and had its own constituency of dedicated fans. Dhoni mostly turned out for Durga Sporting and Sangha Shree, two popular local clubs. Both Dhoni and Robin played for Durga Sporting, which was owned by one Tunu Singh, who also happened to be Dhoni's landlord during his stay in Golkhuli. The matches were played across the city, among which were Traffic, BNR, Silver Jubilee and Higli High School Grounds.

This form of cricket was high voltage drama. Talented batsmen, who had gained some expertise in that format, could hit the ball high and hard. Since the pitch was shorter in length, the lighter ball reached the bat at a much faster pace. To negotiate that kind of bowling, the batsman needed to have quick reflexes, a quality Dhoni certainly didn't lack. In no time, he became the king of 'khep' cricket.

During that era, Dhoni could barely afford a modest lifestyle. He didn't own a bike, although Robin, whom Dhoni addressed as Kallu, did. However, because of his passion for bikes, he ended up riding while his friend and SER captain rode the pillion when they went to play 'khep' matches. Robin remembers, 'On holidays and weekends, we would ride down to small villages to play matches. 'Khep' cricket was very exciting since the match moved at a very fast pace. Also, one could travel light and no extra cricketing kit needed to be carried. Just a bat would suffice for the tournament.'

Dhoni played most of his 'khep' cricket matches for Durga Sporting, but he never charged any money on the condition that Singh would give a one-room accommodation to him and his friends in Golkhuli without charging any rent. The room

JOURNEY TO KHARAGPUR • 35

that was given to him did not have any attached toilet. Hence, Dhoni had to use a common one. He bathed in the open by standing next to a well. But having a free room seemed good enough. While playing for other teams, he charged a princely sum of ₹2,000 per match. Most others were paid anything between ₹100 and ₹1,000. The player's fee was in keeping with his popularity and talent. In such a situation, Dhoni being the master blaster worked in his favour.

The interesting thing is, Dhoni never haggled with team managers over money. He knew his worth since his sheer presence in a match drew huge crowds. Whenever he got out cheaply, ninety per cent of the visitors went back home disappointed. Had he asked for a few hundred rupees more, most managers would have complied without asking a single question. However, he stayed away from bargaining, played every match passionately, enjoyed every moment on the field—just as the crowds watching him in action did—and went back home.

Kharagpur saw Dhoni as a TTE who had come from Ranchi and enthralled the city for a few years. Cricket lovers who had watched him play for the SER and 'khep' cricket lovers cannot stop comparing the man of today with how he used to be so many years ago. After he had risen to prominence in Indian cricket, *The Telegraph* reported that his friends were full of praise for the down-to-earth manner in which he conducts himself off the field even today. The newspaper shared a story in its report: 'Once, after he received the man-of-the-match trophy from Bengal spinner Shiv Sagar Singh at the tournament finals in Panskura in 2002, Mahi was asked to say something. But he just told the organiser apologetically: "Mujhe bolna nahin aata (I can't make a speech)." This same guy is so articulate now. His speech is so polished. It's like magic,' says Sinha (Prasenjit Sinha, who played 'khep' tournaments with him.)'[3]

Those who knew him in Kharagpur experience what change means when they talk about their association with the Indian captain. There are times when they become susceptible to sarcastic comments of others who don't know them. After Dhoni had played for India and hit that majestic knock of 148 against Pakistan in the ODI, Baghada and Robin had gone to Meerut to pick up some good quality cricket equipment.

After completing their purchase, the two of them were going back to the hotel where they were staying. On their way back, they saw a small group of people who had gathered outside a shop selling electronic goods. The owner of the shop had switched on a television set while a match was on, a commonplace strategy used by sellers with the hope that a few among those would walk into the store and check out what all is on sale. That seldom happens yet the seller implements this approach day after day.

Baghada and Robin being cricket addicts slowed down the moment they saw a match being shown on the shop's television set. What heightened their curiosity was that Dhoni was at the crease. So they decided to stand along with the others and enjoy a few overs. Both Baghada and Robin watched and chatted as Dhoni continued to hit the bowlers without showing any sign of slowing down.

Cricket lovers standing around Baghada and Robin somehow figured out that the two of them knew Dhoni.

[3]'Mahi of Midnapore,' *The Telegraph*, Rith Basu, 9 November 2008. http://www.telegraphindia.com/1081109/jsp/calcutta/story_10081820. jsp (accessed 17 December 2014).

Somebody asked Robin if he had met him. Robin responded by saying that he had played with Dhoni, an honest answer which was met with disbelief. Robin, who could have stopped the conversation right there, took it further and pointed towards Baghada to inform the crowd that the latter 'had coached him.' The moment he said that, everybody started laughing. For them, Baghada and Robin were just a part of an ordinary crowd that was watching a cricket match outside a shop. Dhoni had turned into somebody who was meant to be seen and met only when one was extraordinarily lucky. Dhoni was way beyond the reach of the ordinary person who couldn't play with him or coach him. Hence, anybody making such tall claims had to be a liar.

Today, the Indian captain has very little time for anything except cricket. But when he meets his friends, he is the same old chap. When Robin met him after he had started playing for Team India, he took out his cell phone so that he could click a photograph with Dhoni. A clearly astonished Dhoni asked him why he wanted to prioritize a photograph over chatting with him. Robin kept the cell phone away, having understood that his now-famous friend had no idea of what a photograph with him meant. Dhoni hadn't changed a bit, which made Robin proud and happy.

Dhoni hasn't been to Kharagpur and spent time with his friends for a while now. However, *The Times of India* published a report that evoked a fond memory of how he had dined with his friends during his last visit to the town. A friend recollects that all of them stole into 'a compartment of the Gitanjali Express when it was in the car-shed and had dinner.' His former captain of Sanga Shree, Siddhartha Chatterjee, said,

'Every time any of us texts him, he calls back. That's our Dhoni.'[4]

Dhoni would eventually leave his job in Kharagpur in late 2004. In mid-2005, he joined the Indian Airlines. The town where he played many matches now hosts the M.S. Dhoni Museum at the SERSA Stadium, which contains memorabilia including a bat he used to play with and even his wicketkeeping gloves. Interestingly, the museum also showcases his appointment letter with the SER. That he has been honoured thus is hardly surprising, the very thought of the budding cricketer of yesteryears being an exquisite memory for his 'khep' cricket fans.

What no museum can show is Dhoni's ambition even while he was playing for minor teams. Like many gifted cricketers, he always yearned to play for India and was preparing himself for his eventual goal. Time has flown. He has achieved his target, but the story is far from over. The most discussed cricketer in India after Sachin Tendulkar, Dhoni as a skipper has surpassed his former counterpart Sourav Ganguly in terms of the reams of newsprint and hours on television that have been dedicated to the analyses of his accomplishments and shortcomings as a leader. He symbolizes the experience of the modern-day Indian cricketing megastar for whom criticism and adulation are never far apart.

In Ranchi as well as in Kharagpur, Dhoni was never known for his leadership qualities. That being the case, did he think like a captain before he became one? Talking to *ESPNcricinfo. com*, Dhoni had admitted, 'Not really. It came to me quite late.

---

[4]'Town that saw Dhoni as a ticket collector,' *The Times of India*, 3 April 2011. http://epaper.timesofindia.com/Repository/ml.asp?Ref=VE9JQk cvMjAxMS8wNC8wMy9BcjAxNDAw (accessed 17 December 2014).

Till class 10 or 11, I wouldn't really go up front and say things. I would wait and watch. As the wicketkeeper, you always are in a position where the captain comes up to you and asks different things. In a way it goes on in the subconscious. Being a wicketkeeper really helped me more than anything. Whatever was in my mind, I used to speak. I never used to just go through the motions and follow whatever the skipper said. Whatever I felt, I used to say, but if I was not sure, I wouldn't really answer. I didn't believe in confusing the captain more. I was pretty clear in my thoughts and it came to me gradually, watching the game from behind the stumps—how it progresses, how it is played in different parts of the world.'[5]

How he has been leading the team is a must-have part of the Dhoni narrative. Before he wore the India colours, however, there were struggles, disappointments and failures too. Only after that would he see his bright moment under the sun.

---

[5]'If there's commitment, that's victory for me,' *ESPNcricinfo.com*, Personal Interview by Siddhartha Vaidyanathan and Nagraj Gollapudi, 24 March 2008. http://www.espncricinfo.com/magazine/content/story/343750. html (accessed 17 December 2014).

PROMISES AND HIGHS

INTERNATIONAL DEBUT AT the age of twenty-three is not exactly young for India. But Dhoni had to wriggle his way into the side after being tried and tested at every level. In the domestic circuit, he had played for Bihar and Jharkhand, both small teams, whose gifted players were vulnerable to getting lost in the crowd simply because their squads didn't perform well. In the domestic circuit, therefore, he had to keep his chin up and wage a lonely battle before breaking into the Indian team.

In the 1998-99 season, he played in the Cooch Behar Trophy, an U-19 tournament consisting of three-day matches. Bihar didn't do well, but Dhoni managed to retain his place. In the following season, he also played for the East Zone in the C.K. Nayudu Trophy, a zonal level U-19 tournament of one-dayers. In the Cooch Behar Trophy that year, Bihar surprised many pundits by reaching the finals. Dhoni had done his bit—both behind the wickets and in front of them—by scoring three half centuries on the way to the final. When Bihar met Punjab in the final at the Keenan Stadium in Jamshedpur, the entire team was shell-shocked by what followed.

Batting first on a good wicket, Bihar scored 357, with Dhoni hitting his way to 84 in quick time. But Punjab's response had to be experienced to be believed. The team batted for well over 200 overs and scored a massive 839 for the loss of 5 wickets!. Elegant southpaw and his future Team India colleague Yuvraj Singh scored 358, which was one more than the sum total of Bihar's score! Bihar was trounced, and a young Dhoni was heartbroken. Sanjeev remembers, 'When he got back home, he was very sad. He had given the match his everything, yet Punjab won easily.' The boy who believed in winning had failed to do it for his state in a crucial match. He was disappointed; yet, in a handful of days, he had learned that not all important results would favour his team.

Facts indicate that the beginning of Dhoni's career in domestic cricket was marred by inconsistency. If his first-class record makes for decent but unspectacular reading even today—124 matches, 6970 runs at an average of 37.07 with nine centuries and forty-seven half centuries—it is only fair to conclude that he needed far more challenging situations to excel as a batsman. For that to happen, however, he had to play for the state team first. That happened when he managed to sneak into the Bihar squad for the Ranji Trophy in January 2000.

The team was captained by Sunil Kumar who, despite his modest first-class record, was an important and highly respected player. Since Kumar was advised to let go of his keeping duties, Dhoni took up the role of a wicketkeeper-batsman whose first outing was against Assam in Jamshedpur.

Among the most ordinary teams in the Ranji Trophy, Assam crashed to a 191-run defeat against Bihar, a relatively stronger outfit. In his very first match, Dhoni played his part fairly well, scoring 40 in the first innings in which Bihar scored 258. In the second innings, when the team needed to score as rapidly as possible to set Assam a very tough target, Dhoni remained not out on 68. Assam had to chase a decent target of 355, but the last batsman was sent back to the pavilion with the score reading 163. For young Dhoni, the debut was a happy one. A weak opposition notwithstanding, he had performed well in his first-class debut. The team had won. What more could he have asked for?

That he had broken into the state side was a huge step forward. In an extensive interview to *ESPNcricinfo.com*, he would confess, 'To me, even to get into my Ranji Trophy side was a big thing. Fortunately, we had a selector who believed in youngsters. We qualified for the U-19 that year and made it to the finals, so there was a big change and all of a sudden we saw five youngsters getting into the Bihar Ranji squad. That was a start. Bihar was considered a small state and for you to be a part of the zonal team, especially to be in the XI, it is tough. You have to perform consistently for that. So every stage, wherever you are playing, it gets a bit tough. You have to be very consistent.'[6] That season, Bihar qualified for the Super League. But neither Bihar nor Dhoni performed well. While the state lost all its matches, Dhoni who had a horrible run with the bat barely managed to score 175 in eight innings.

A senior cricketer who shall remain unnamed says, 'Right from the beginning of the career, his talent was very much in evidence. But there were two major causes for worry during

---

[6]'If there's commitment, that's victory for me,' *ESPNcricinfo.com*, Interview by Siddhartha Vaidyanathan and Nagraj Gollapudi, 24 March 2008. http://www.espncricinfo.com/magazine/content/story/343750.html (accessed 17 December 2014).

his first season with the state side. First, he threw his wicket away on too many occasions. Also, he was not a particularly polished wicketkeeper. He stood behind the stumps and did well when mediocre bowlers did the job. Watching him keep, one had every reason to doubt that he wouldn't be able to play the role while keeping at a higher level.'

The same cricketer admits that Dhoni emerged as a far more mature wicketkeeper-batsman in the following season. He says, 'When he turned out for his state, I was pleasantly surprised to see that he had become a far better keeper. As a batsman, he continued to be as aggressive as ever. From the outside, it did seem that he had been working really hard.' Although Dhoni has never stated this in any interview, it is possible that his experience and exposure in the previous season had allowed him to observe his counterparts from the other teams. He would have identified some of the loopholes in his batting and wicketkeeping techniques and endeavoured to rectify them by spending long hours at the nets. Appreciated for his work ethic since the day he picked up the bat and wore those big gloves for his school team and desperate to wear the Team India cap one day, he refused to reconcile with weaknesses. That showed.

That year, he represented East Zone against South Zone in the Deodhar Trophy one-day tournament. In January 2001 came the first big moment of Dhoni's career at Kolkata's Eden Gardens where he was playing against Bengal in a Ranji Trophy league match. Bengal batted first and put up 608 runs for the loss of 5 wickets. Facing a mammoth target, Bihar had to evade the prospects of facing a follow-on. It failed as they merely managed to score 323. However, Dhoni made a huge impact, scoring a responsible and intelligently crafted 114 not out. Although Bihar had to follow on, the match eventually ended in a draw.

History repeated itself in the 2001-02 season. Bihar was unable to go past the first hurdle in both the Ranji formats— the four-day matches and the one-dayers. In the 2002-03 season, when the Plate and the Elite system were introduced in the Ranji Trophy, Bihar lost all their four finished matches to languish at the bottom of Group B in the Plate division. In the one-dayers, they did better by finishing second to Bengal with Dhoni scoring three half-centuries. Playing in the Deodhar Trophy for the East Zone, Dhoni hit two more fifties in three matches. With such performances accompanied by the significance of his playing role, Dhoni couldn't have escaped the attention of the national selectors for a long time. And indeed, he did not.

27 January 2004. At the Keenan Stadium in Jamshedpur in the Deodhar Trophy against the Central Zone, Dhoni, who was playing as the opener with Deep Dasgupta keeping wickets, scored a delightfully aggressive knock of 114 which played a significant role in taking the East Zone to a formidable 324 for 4 from 50 overs. Faced with such a target, the Central Zone collapsed for 182 runs with only Jai Prakash Yadav managing to score a half-century.

In the three previous ties, Dhoni had made 25 runs against the West Zone in a low-scoring match that the East Zone somehow managed to win by one wicket. Against the South Zone, there was a strange statistical coincidence as, once again, the East Zone won by one wicket with one ball to spare. Dhoni scored a quick 65 from 60 balls. Against the North Zone, he made 40 as Devang Gandhi (75 not out) and Kiran Powar (79 not out) guided the East Zone to an easy win by eight wickets. But the match against the Central Zone was the final for all practical purposes. Dhoni was the star in it. More importantly, not only did he score at a very quick pace, but he also stayed on till the team's score had reached 282. Commenting on the knock, *Sportstar* observed, 'East Zone's opening batsman, M.S. Dhoni's 114 versus Central was the best individual knock of the championship which also propelled the team to post the tournament's record total of 324 for four in 50 overs.'[7] Fortunately, for Indian cricket, Dhoni was destined for much bigger things in life.

The Duleep Trophy that followed introduced an important change. For the first time in its history, a team from abroad had been invited to participate—the guests being the England 'A' team which had promising players such as Kevin Pietersen, Michael Lumb and attacking wicketkeeper-batsman Matt Prior. Dhoni was selected to play as an opener once more, with Dasgupta keeping the wickets. Certain cricket experts are of the view that Dhoni should have been asked to keep wickets instead of Dasgupta who had been holding that position for a little too long. But the fact is that he stayed in the team with Dhoni playing as a specialist opener.

Playing at the Gandhi Sports Complex in Amritsar, the East Zone won the tie by 93 runs. Although Shib Sundar Das (124) was the only batsman to reach the three-figure mark in the match, Dhoni's brief and breezy performances with the bat—that included a fine 52 in the first innings—was noticed by one and all.

---

[7]'East Zone emerges unscathed,' *Sportstar*, S. Sabanayakan, 21-27 February 2004. http://www.sportstaronnet.com/tss2708/stories/ 20040 221000504400.htm (accessed 17 December 2014).

Dasgupta was eventually dropped for the final against the North Zone at the Punjab Cricket Association in Mohali, and Dhoni was asked to keep wickets as well as open the batting. For the North Zone, Yuvraj Singh scored centuries in both the innings, his 148 in the second being a particularly destructive knock. Chasing down 409 in the fourth innings was going to be tough. But Dhoni was in a different frame of mind. After scoring 21 in the first innings, Dhoni went on a rampage in the second, blasting 60 from 47 balls. The East Zone eventually lost the match by 59 runs.

One dark spot during Dhoni's rise as a cricketer was his appearance for selection in the Railways Ranji Trophy team trials held at the Karnail Singh Stadium in Delhi. He was neglected and rejected. He would go on to tell *ESPNcricinfo.com* later, 'I don't really know the exact year when the trials were held at the Karnail Singh Stadium [Railways' home ground, in Delhi]. Before that, I think, Railways had done really well. I was part of the trials, I played a few balls, I kept wickets, and I was turned down. It never really bothered me. Later, when I got selected for the Duleep Trophy, I got a call from Railways asking me to play for them. I said, "No, no, I'm not coming." That's what happened. Perhaps I was rude or whatever, but it had a big impact on me as well.'[8]

If that incident made him a mentally strong person, his mindset of a gutsy cricketer evolved because of his battles in the domestic circuit while playing for an ordinary state side.

---

[8]'If there's commitment, that's victory for me,' *ESPNcricinfo.com*, Interview by Siddhartha Vaidyanathan and Nagraj Gollapudi, 24 March 2008. http://www.espncricinfo.com/magazine/content/story/343750.html (accessed 17 December 2014).

Midway through his domestic career, he had to confront a lot of criticism for being a little too belligerent for his own good. But while he did mature with experience which reflected in his ability to control an innings and check his pace of scoring, if any such need arose, he refused to abandon his naturally attacking style of batsmanship. From time to time, the helicopter shot was in view. He hit flat sixes with strokes that resembled smashes executed with clinical perfection in lawn tennis. He was born to be unconventional. He continued to be unconventional. In his style of batting, there was no fundamental change.

Being in the India 'A' side within the next few months was inevitable. After his century against Pakistan 'A' in his fourth appearance, few doubted that the young man from Ranchi would play for India very soon. When one looks at it today, the Dhoni story as we now know, was bound to begin.

THE JOURNEY BEGINS

EVERY ASPIRING SPORTSMAN has some special moments in his career. During his days in the domestic circuit, Dhoni—because of his state's obscure cricketing background—needed several of them to make a mark. Once he had found his way into the India 'A' side, his first swashbuckling innings came at the Gymkhana Club in Nairobi on 16 August 2004. India 'A' captained by Sairaj Bahutule was playing against Pakistan 'A' led by Misbah-ul-Haq at the Kenya triangular tournament in which the third participant was the host nation.

Batting first, India 'A' suffered an early setback when opener Dheeraj Jadhav was dismissed for 10 runs. In came Dhoni, who had been assigned to bat at number three. He and the other opener, Gautam Gambhir, tore into the Pakistani attack and shared a 207 run stand which came off just 32 overs. Gambhir was the more aggressive one in that match, taking only 113 balls to score 122 runs. Dhoni scored 120 from 122 balls, which included ten boundaries and two massive sixes. The two of them ensured a solid foundation which eventually took the India 'A' team to 330 for 6 from 50 overs. Pakistan 'A,' who had been reduced to 100 for 5, never quite looked like coming close to the target. They were eventually bundled out for 209, leading to an easy India 'A' victory by 121 runs.

In many ways, Dhoni's innings was an indication that he had finally arrived on the big stage. He showed a certain degree of maturity while mixing aggressive strokes with defensive ones. He ran incredibly fast between the wickets, which prompted Misbah into thinking about single-saving strategies to stop Dhoni from scoring. He did not try to outshine Gambhir, who batted beautifully and scored most of the runs in their partnership.

Gambhir got out with the score at 245, but Dhoni stayed there until the score had reached 306. When Ramesh Powar came out to bat at number four, Dhoni played a steady hand as the newcomer to the crease went on a rampage and scored 33 from 19 balls. Dhoni on his part didn't wish to give it away; yet, he kept on scoring at a fast clip. He was not the quintessential pinch hitter. Instead, he was capable of scoring fast while controlling an innings. Of course, Dhoni would take some time before he finally took on that role seriously and rose to prominence as the best finisher in the shorter version of the game. But, he needed to take that crucial step upward and get a chance to play for the 'real thing,' an opportunity that would present itself when he would represent India against Bangladesh in December 2004.

Dhoni's emergence in Indian cricket was inevitable. Between 2000 and 2005, Team India had used as many as eleven wicketkeepers. Considering that the role of the man behind the wickets is such an important one, India's inability to find a person who seemed good enough to be there for a long-enough period was a major reason of grief for both the selectors and cricket lovers.

The drama, if one can call it that, began in the 1999-2000 Indian tour of Australia. MSK Prasad, who kept wickets in the

Test series, flattered to deceive. Samir Dighe kept in the ODI tri-series. Rahul Dravid played the occasional keeper time and again, which showed that Indian selectors were hunting for a permanent solution without being able to find any. So, the hunt was on. Nayan Mongia, who had been dropped, was back for a brief while in 2001. Deep Dasgupta was another chosen one. Vijay Dahiya was unconvincing. Ajay Ratra appeared to be a decent option while playing against the West Indies in 2002. But he got injured in the same year and was replaced by Parthiv Patel. Patel was an average keeper, but a potentially useful contributor with the bat. After his disastrous show in Australia followed by another bad display against the touring Australians, he was replaced by Dinesh Karthik.

Among those wicketkeepers was Syed Saba Karim. Like Dhoni, who was born in Ranchi in the then undivided Bihar, Karim was from Patna, the capital of the state at that time. Way back during India's 1989 tour to the West Indies, Karim, was chosen as the reserve wicketkeeper. He didn't get to play a single international match. After a seven-year-long wait, Karim got an opportunity to tour South Africa in 1996. But his batting form let him down and out he went. Still, the fighter in him remained alive and he was picked for the South African tour to India in 2000. It appeared that Karim would wear the keeping gloves for India for sometime. But, it was during his only Test against Bangladesh in the same year that an Anil Kumble delivery inflicted an eye injury on Karim and ended his career.

Dhoni took his first baby step when the India 'A' team went on a tour of Zimbabwe and Kenya. He accompanied the team as the second wicketkeeper. Although He had played in an outing as an opener with Karthik as the specialist keeper, he got his first real opportunity only after the latter was summoned for the England tour. Now, he had to prove his worth in the tri-nation tournament during the Kenyan leg of the tour featuring India 'A,' Pakistan 'A' and Kenya as the three participants.

Neither India 'A' nor Dhoni fared well in the opening match, with India 'A' losing to Kenya by 20 runs. Dhoni got out for 8, not the sort of score he would have been pleased with. But the start had been made. The strong lad in him had to move on.

Just one day later, lady luck smiled at Dhoni. In a fascinating reversal of fortunes, India 'A' defeated Pakistan 'A' led by Misbah-ul-Haq by four wickets with Dhoni scoring 70, a Man of the Match-winning performance. In their third outing, this time against Kenya once again, India 'A' did not allow the Kenyan team to cause another upset. They crushed the comparatively inexperienced hosts by ten wickets. Dhoni was responsible for five dismissals behind the stumps, his equally if not more important role in the game. Then came the match against Pakistan 'A' in which he and opener Gautam Gambhir shared a 207 run opening wicket partnership and took the game away from Pakistan with ease. After that performance, people started looking at Dhoni more seriously than ever before.

After defeating Kenya by six wickets in which Dhoni scored 30, India qualified for the finals. However, one more league match against arch rival Pakistan was yet to take place. When it did, Dhoni was on fire. He hit nine boundaries and five massive sixes in his unbeaten knock of 119 not out, another Man of the Match-winning performance. This time India 'A' defeated Pakistan by eight wickets. For Pakistan, skipper Misbah-ul-Haq scored 106. But on a Dhoni-dominated day, his innings was a wasted effort. Another encounter against Pakistan in the finals resulted in yet another easy six-wicket win for India.

Although Dhoni scored only 15, he was quite easily the player to watch out for. He scored 362 runs at an average of 72.40 in the tri-series, which was nothing short of fantastic. Besides, he proved his usefulness behind the stumps. Not only was he not prone to blunders, he also pulled off some excellent dismissals. Dhoni had done what was expected of him—and a lot more.

While the Dhoni story was beginning to unfold, he was, off the field, the same shy lad who rarely spoke. During dinner time, he used to order his food in his hotel room. But he was proud of his hair, which was at that time straight, long and had a deep brown colour. When his teammates suggested that he should change his hairstyle, he refused. In fact, he strongly believed that there would come a time when others would copy his hairstyle. And so he would tell his teammates. It was a non-cricketing prophecy which would eventually turn out to be true, with many Indian youngsters imitating his hairstyle. Among them is a young Jharkhand southpaw who hasn't quite made a mark in Indian cricket but is gifted and young enough to make a comeback. He responds to the name of Saurabh Tiwary.

Karthik's flop shows with the bat was the main reason why the Ranchi boy debuted in the ODI series against Bangladesh. Those matches proved to be tougher than one had imagined. The home team was known to spring surprises in the shorter version, and that 'almost' happened in the first game in Chittagong on 23 December 2004.

Batting first, India slumped to 45 for 3. Interestingly, two batsmen got out for ducks: Dhoni and Ganguly. Responding to India's total of 245 for 8, Bangladesh reached 234 for 8 in their 50 overs, allowing the visitors to take a 1-0 lead in the series. India won without Dhoni having the sort of beginning he was looking for.

The second match at Dhaka proved to be good news for Bangladesh. India failed to chase a modest score of 229 for 9 and fell 15 runs short. Once again, Dhoni failed to perform with the bat, scoring just 12 runs. Behind the stumps his first victim was Nafees Iqbal who was caught off an Ajit Agarkar's delivery. The result showed that the decision to test the bench strength by resting Tendulkar, Dravid, Harbhajan and all-rounder Irfan Pathan had boomeranged. For the third series-decider, India fielded the strongest possible side, which helped them gallop to 348 for 5. Dhoni, who faced just two balls and hit the first six of his Team India career, was excellent behind the stumps with three catches and two stumpings, which made his day.

The young man from Ranchi had managed to break into the team. But that certainly wasn't enough. He needed to consolidate his position, and he needed to do that fast. Against Bangladesh, he had managed to do well as a keeper without being able to make any impact with the bat. Karthik, while playing for India, had also been more than efficient behind the wickets. Patel had been dropped, but he wasn't far behind in the race either. For a change, India had a problem of plenty.

Who was the best of the lot? That was the answer everyone was looking for.

148: JUST A 'ONE DAY' WONDER?

THE STATE OF Jharkhand was carved out of an undivided Bihar on 15 November 2000. But Jharkhand's cricket team made its debut in Ranji Trophy almost five years later. Dhoni was one of the few players to have represented both Bihar and Jharkhand. He had sharpened his skills while playing for Bihar and got an opportunity to play for Jharkhand after the Bangladesh series had ended. Interestingly, the captain of India never ever captained his state side.

His season with his newly formed state side which played in the Plate Division and also for the East Zone proved to be a productive one. Playing against the West Zone in the Deodhar Trophy, he scored a century. Playing for his state in the Ranji Trophy, he scored a ton against Odisha and another against Haryana in the Plate semifinal, which Jharkhand lost. As a player, who has always believed that playing the game is important, no matter at what level, Dhoni sparkled in the 2004-05 season which saw him turn out for Jharkhand for the last time. He never found the time to go back to his state team thereafter.

Although his beginning hadn't been remarkable, the simple fact that he had been able to make it to the Indian team made Dhoni a big star in his hometown. But the young Dhoni remained unfazed by all the adulation around him. He did not forget his favourite joints—Chashme Shahi Restaurant and Madhuban Dhaba—on the Ranchi–Patna Highway. Every time he went to Ranchi, he met his teachers and friends and also visited the MECON stadium—the ground which helped him nurture his game.

Meanwhile, MECON, the company which Dhoni's father worked for, had found a boy to be proud of. There would come a time when the consultancy giant would make its best efforts to ensure that Dhoni and his family stayed on in Shyamali colony by offering them a spacious home which is today a destination for every Dhoni fan visiting Ranchi.

In spite of Dhoni's performance with the bat in the domestic circuit, Karthik got the nod ahead of him for the Test series. But as a former selector says, 'Karthik seemed to be a better choice because there were expectations that he could build an innings once he got used to the challenges of international cricket. Dhoni, on the other hand, was a destroyer. He could be expected to play a destructive innings but not those in which the batsman had to be patient and build his knock brick by brick. That made him a more useful ODI batsman.'

During the Test series against Pakistan, Karthik scored a big knock of 93 in the second Test. This 93 was a significant knock for him in a match which India won by a massive margin of 195 runs. Pakistan eventually tied the series 1–1. After the Test series, it was ODI time which implied that Dhoni was back in the team.

The first ODI played at Kochi on 2 April 2005, led to an easy Indian win. Dhoni's woes with the bat continued, and he could contribute only 3 runs to the score. Although no published report suggests that Dhoni's batting had become a major cause for concern—it was too early—his first four ODI innings had done nothing to indicate what he was capable of achieving before the second match in Visakhapatnam.

Even though the performances were not in Dhoni's favour, Sourav Ganguly was convinced about the talent of the lad who had emerged from a humble background and conquered huge odds to reach where he had. Known for his ability to spot and back young talents, Ganguly—who had gifted prodigies like Harbhajan Singh, Yuvraj Singh and Virender Sehwag to Indian cricket—understood the need for supporting youngsters whose wealth of talent didn't deserve to remain confined to the obscurity of domestic circuit. Although he would explain his decision to send Dhoni at number three later, the Indian skipper decided to gamble in Vishakapatnam that day.

At that time, Pakistan's bowling was nowhere near good. What the team did have was a reasonably decent bowling line-up comprising the likes of Mohammed Sami, Naved-ul-Hassan, Abdul Razzaq, Shahid Afridi and Mohammed Hafeez. Batting first, India lost Tendulkar early. Surprising the opposition, Dhoni walked in. It turned out to be a knockout punch.

Indifferent to the dismissal of Tendulkar, Sehwag, who was at the other end, was batting in the only way he did and could: as an assassin who knew no full stops. In 10.2 overs, Sehwag and Dhoni added 96 runs to the Indian score. After scoring 74 from 40 balls, which included twelve boundaries and two sixes, Sehwag got out with the score reading 122. During this partnership, Dhoni hadn't been the silent partner. But Sehwag very clearly was the man on rampage.

After Sehwag got out, Ganguly was the next man in. Far from being his lordly self, the captain impacted the scoring rate by managing a meagre 9 from 22 balls. Dhoni was then joined by Rahul Dravid. Until sometime ago, Dravid had kept wickets for India, a role which hardly suited him. In front of him that day stood a genuine wicketkeeper-batsman who had scored at a decent clip apart from sharing a fine partnership with Sehwag after which Ganguly had brought down the run rate. Dravid was the epitome of near-perfect technique. Each stroke that Dhoni hit defied the norms of technical perfection. Dravid on the other hand, was the perfect craftsman. Dhoni sought to demolish the opposition into submission. Dravid knew the art of consolidation. The contrast was great to watch.

Dravid played fluently without taking any unnecessary risk to score 52 from 59 deliveries. Dhoni unleashed such a huge range of strokes that every spectator in the ground was astounded. Pakistani bowlers tried everything they could, but in vain. On the one hand, none of them were remotely comparable to their illustrious predecessors—such as Imran Khan, Wasim Akram, Waqar Younis and Abdul Qadir—who had crafted many historic wins against India. On the other hand, the fact that none of them had seen this young man at his devastating best made bowling to him with any specific gameplan impossible for them. Ganguly sat smiling inside the pavilion, watching his young prodigy wreak havoc.

Although Dhoni's 148 was the highest ever scored by an Indian wicketkeeper-batsman and it also happened to be his first century against an international opposition, what was noticeable was his calmness which eventually became the hallmark of Dhoni, the captain. *ESPNcricinfo.com* observed, 'His scorching hits in the V off the fast bowlers and lofted sixes off the spinner demoralized the opposition no end. Nothing could stop Dhoni, and even when all the players on the field hit the ground in flash as a swarm of bees came into the ground, he stood tall, casually sauntering about his crease, almost wondering what the fuss was all about.'[9]

Riding piggyback on Dhoni's and Sehwag's knocks, India piled up 356 for the loss of nine wickets. Pakistan tried to chase it down but fell short of 58 runs. Addressing the post match conference, Ganguly explained his strategy. 'When I looked at the wicket in the morning, it looked like it would crumble quite quickly, and might not even be good for batting for the first 50 overs. So the toss was absolutely crucial, and once we won it, it was important that we made as many runs as possible in the first 15 overs. That's why we made the decision to send Dhoni in and he played fantastically well.' After the win at Visakhapatnam, India led 2-0 in the ODI series. That definitely put them in a favourable position.

Jamshedpur's Keenan stadium was viewed as an iconic institution in an undivided Bihar before Jharkhand came into being. Dhoni had played many matches there during his pre-Team India days. But the third match against Pakistan was his first international match in the city where he was seen as a local boy who had made everybody proud by playing a mind-blowing knock against their nation's arch-rival a few days ago. Needless to say, his hordes of fans were sure that he would play another big one, an expectation Dhoni failed to fulfill.

Pakistan destroyed India with a 106-run win. Bolstered by opener Salman Butt's century and Shoaib Malik's 75, they reached 319. India, in response, crumbled for a mere 213.

---

[9]'Dhoni shines in Indian win,' *ESPNcricinfo.com*, Anand Vasu, 5 April 2005. http://www.espncricinfo.com/ci/content/story/143829.html (accessed 17 December 2014).

Irfan Pathan batting lower down in the order was the highest scorer with 64 runs. Dhoni, who played at number three, tried too much too soon. In spite of Sehwag, Tendulkar and Ganguly's loss, he failed to adapt himself to the requirements of the situation and lost his wicket after scoring 28 runs. Had Dhoni been in a similar situation today, he would have paced his innings in a far better and shrewd manner. At that time, his youth and inexperience brought about his downfall. When he lost his wicket, the spectators, who were chanting his name all through fell silent.

It was after the match ended that Ganguly's move took everybody by surprise. Summoned by the match referee to explain his team's slow over rate—he would have to serve out a ban later—the Indian skipper sent Dhoni ahead of the others to take questions during the post match conference attended by local journalists as well as those who had come from other cities. When asked whether he was disappointed at his personal performance in front of the home crowd, Dhoni said, 'Look, international cricket isn't that simple. It's tough competition and their fast bowlers bowled really well.' In response to whether the team will discuss a strategy to counter the bowling, he answered, 'We will certainly look at it during the next team meeting. It also depends a lot on the pitches that we get in the coming games.'

Such innocuous questions were easy to answer. The difficult one was responding to the question about the mood in the dressing room. The young man's response was a crisp one. 'The boys are not shattered. We have won two of the matches so far. They just played very well today and congratulations to them.' Here was a cricketer who had just walked into the team. And he was already talking about his teammates as 'the boys'—an expression that was usually used by the skipper or some senior player during that period.

The toughest one to answer was whether Tendulkar's and Ganguly's poor forms were affecting the team's performance. Dhoni reasoned, 'Not a question of pressure. Sehwag had been making runs at the top of the order, and there was not much time for the middle-order batsmen to do anything. This was the first chance for them.' The journalist, who had asked about his skipper's performance, hadn't posed a merely tricky question. It was a cruel one, since the man who had been sent out to respond had played in just about a handful of ODIs. Throughout the conference, Dhoni spoke with a smile and an easy calm. It seemed as if an experienced customer with hundred ODIs behind him had been asked to represent the team in the skipper's absence.

The fourth match in Ahmedabad was a classic example of an ideal Indo-Pak clash. India scored 315 for 6, an innings in which Dhoni made two contributions. He scored a composed 47 from 64 balls, which certainly wasn't typical of him. Besides, he was content to play the second fiddle to his idol Sachin Tendulkar in their second-wicket partnership of 129 runs. Pakistan chased down the target in a last-ball finish and the series was tied at 2-2. After going down in the last two matches in which Dhoni's performance was hardly spectacular, India lost the series 4-2.

The bigger news, and some would say a terrible one, was that the verdict of this series coincided with the end of the tenure of New Zealand cricketer-turned-coach John Wright who, along with Ganguly, had been playing a very important role in turning the Indian cricket team into a cohesive and successful unit. Among those who had played in all the six matches, Dhoni was at the second spot after Rahul Dravid by scoring 261 runs at an average of 43.50. This sounds decent on paper. The reality, however, was that his tally and average did not reflect his consistency.

More than half of his runs had been generated by one spectacular knock. He had got starts in a few innings without being able to convert them into substantial scores. He had showcased his potential in one knock and displayed exemplary calmness and analytical insight while addressing a post match conference. That seemed to suggest that the future was in good hands—and not only because of his glovework, which would mature considerably in times to come.

After Wright's tenure ended, Indian cricket experienced a tectonic shift. A new coach had to be hired. Sourav Ganguly insisted on the selection of Greg Chappell, the feisty Australian ex-skipper and a batting legend of his times. Ganguly's choice had been prompted by Chappell's guidance towards his mental approach that had enabled him to play an epical knock of 144 in Brisbane against Australia in the first Test of the 2003-04 tour. Unable to foresee any possibility of a destructive impact on his own career, Ganguly's choice was a manifestation of his gratitude.

For a young Dhoni, who had played in a handful of matches during Wright's tenure, the Australian newcomer as a coach was just another person who would guide him. What he had to do was surpass his rivals, consolidate his position in the ODI team and also be part of the Test side. He had been divine at Visakhapatnam. History had to repeat itself and he had to make it happen, with or without Chappell.

CONQUEST AND PROGRESS

31 OCTOBER 2005. Many would say that this day was the defining moment of Dhoni's career. His explosion with the bat at Visakhapatnam had been well and truly sensational. But Dhoni needed to convince the nation—and more importantly, himself—that he was capable of hitting those big ones against any opposition, and that too, more than just once.

It happened that day.

India were playing Sri Lanka in the third match of the ODI series in Jaipur. On a batsman-friendly pitch, Sri Lanka, who batted first, put up a formidable score of 298 for 4 on the board, helped by Kumara Sangakkara's 138 and Mahela Jayawardene's 71. How would India approach the target? That was the big question whose answer every Indian cricket fan was waiting for. The Sri Lankans had a seriously good bowling line-up led by Muttiah Muralitharan and Chaminda Vaas, who were accompanied by paceman Dilhara Fernando and leggie Upul Chandana. On any pitch, in all kinds of conditions, this combination—mainly because of the Murali–Vaas factor—could have been expected to bring any opposition down for far less than the steep target.

Moments after India went in to bat, the crowd in Jaipur fell so silent that one could hear the proverbial pin drop.

Sachin Tendulkar lost his wicket off the fifth delivery of the first over, caught behind for 2 off the bowling of Vaas. Once again, Dhoni, who had experienced quite a few movements up and down in the batting order earlier, was sent in to bat at three. It was a tactic that paid off, and how! The young cricketer's show was aggression at its dazzling best. On a pitch that didn't pose any tricky challenges of pace and bounce, Vaas was nowhere near as potent as he otherwise might have been.

Playing his natural game, Dhoni faced no problem while striding down the pitch to attack non-good length deliveries or hitting through the line when the opportunity was adequately appropriate. Two Vaas deliveries were sent flying for sixes, compelling the Sri Lankan captain Marvan Atapattu to introduce the wily Muralitharan in the eleventh over. But Dhoni, who would go on to acquire a reputation for his ability to pace the innings, played smartly to ensure that Murali didn't bring about his untimely downfall.

With Sehwag (39), who was reduced to a supporting role unlike the Visakhapatnam match in which he had been the attacker during their partnership for the second wicket, Dhoni shared a 92-run partnership. Skipper Dravid walked in to bat after Sehwag's fall and contributed 28, but his contribution was vital since the two of them added 86 for the third wicket. Yuvraj Singh, whose belligerence isn't unknown to anybody, simply stood and watched while chipping in with 18 in their 65-run partnership. For, the day belonged to Dhoni. And who could have known that better than the man batting with him at the other end?

What followed after the introduction of the second

powerplay[10] was a classic illustration of Dhoni's ability to change gears at the right time. After the Sri Lankan skipper Marvan Atapattu took the ball between the seventeenth and the twenty-first overs, the Ranchi boy showed his true colours. During the five-over period, 46 runs were scored. Muralitharan, who eventually gave away 46 runs in his ten-over spell, was handled with exemplary ease. Chandana, who obviously was much easier to deal with, was made to take the aerial route twice. Dhoni started getting severe cramps and was compelled to play with a runner. But he was in no mood to throw his wicket away and scored his last 53 runs with a runner's assistance. His partner at the other end, Venugopal Rao, struggled, scoring a meagre 19 from 39 balls. But Dhoni showed him the way and took India home with a six with 23 balls to spare. He suppressed all apprehensions that 298 would be a challenge for India. Who would have thought that he would overcome the challenge in such an emphatic manner?

Comparing Dhoni's flamboyant knock of 183 not out to Tendulkar's 143 against Australia in Sharjah, skipper Dravid said, 'Anyone who watched it at the ground and on television will agree that it is one of the greatest one-day innings of all time.' As Dravid pointed out, Dhoni had batted for 46 overs after keeping wickets for 50 overs, which made his knock all the more special. Showing no sign of exhaustion, Dhoni remarked, 'The main thing was that I wanted to be there till the end. I wanted to be able to score the winning runs. It was when I reached 160 that I thought of Gilchrist's record of 172. We were a little wary of Muralitharan, he is the best bowler in

---

[10]A powerplay is a term used for certain fielding restrictions in limited-overs and T20 cricket.

their squad, and Rahul and I decided to take singles against him, see him off and attack the other bowlers.' By saying that he had thought of Gilchrist's record, Dhoni admitted that he did target personal glory if not a double century. The good thing was—he had thought of the magical figure only after he had reached 160, an individual score any team will accept wholeheartedly in any version of the game.

Evidently pleased with the young man's growth, the chairman of selectors, Kiran More, told Outlook, 'It was a great innings, an outstanding knock. We do not see too many such innings, perhaps one every five or six years. I watched Saeed Anwar make that 194 against India in Madras, but this was something else. Remember that Dhoni was playing after keeping wickets through the Sri Lanka innings. With his growing experience, he has adopted a sensible approach. He not only plays those big strokes but also takes the ones and twos. His evolution augurs well for himself and the future of Indian cricket.'[11]

Speaking to BBC Sport, former Indian wicketkeeper Vijay Yadav said, 'I think it was a calculated risk taken by the team management. Dhoni's technique, temperament and willingness to stay at the crease was unmatched.'[12]

Wisden Almanack summarized Dhoni's awe-inspiring performance in a striking manner. 'He smacked 15 fours and ten sixes—a record 120 in boundaries—on his way to 183

---

[11]'"Dhoom Dhoom" Dhoni,' *Outlook*, G Rajaraman, 14 November 2005. http://www.outlookindia.com/printarticle.aspx?229224 (accessed 18 December 2014).

[12]'New era for India,' *BBC Sport*, Ayanjit Sen, 1 November 2005. http://news.bbc.co.uk/sport2/hi/cricket/other_international/india/4395994.stm (accessed 18 December 2014).

not out from 145 balls, the sixth-highest score in all one-day internationals and just three short of Tendulkar's Indian record. It was also the highest by a wicketkeeper, eclipsing Adam Gilchrist's 172 against Zimbabwe in 2003-04, and only Sanath Jayasuriya and Shahid Afridi had hit more sixes (11) in an innings. Uninhibited, yet anything but crude, Dhoni's remarkable innings hustled India to victory with 23 balls to spare: fittingly, he ended the match with a six.'[13]

Known to be a thorough gentleman, Sangakkara accepted the loss with the sort of grace that is typically identified with him. 'There's not much to say about it, or describe. You won't see an innings like that again in a long, long time. It was a little gem.'

Before Dhoni's record-breaking masterclass against the Lankans in Jaipur, however, the ebullient wicketkeeper-batsman had played a few other ODI matches. In Chappell's new regime with the Ganguly–Chappell saga yet to unfold, he had gone off to Sri Lanka to play a tri-series featuring the host nation, India and the West Indies. The new coach, whose appetite and proclivity for experimentation was well known, pushed him down to number six in the second tie. In the subsequent match, he was sent in at number four. In the last two matches, including the finals in which Sri Lanka beat India by 18 runs, he returned to the number six position once again.

Dhoni's performance with the bat was absymal as his string of scores showed—2, 15 n.o., 20, 28 n.o. and 7. His keeping was a worrying factor too, the dropping of a crucial Sanath

[13]'India v Sri Lanka, 2005-06,' *Wisden Almanack*, Ramakrishnan Kaushik. http://www.espncricinfo.com/wisdenalmanack/content/story/289060. html (accessed 18 December 2014).

Jayasuriya catch when the opener was on 19—he went on to score 67—playing a big role in India's defeat in the finals. He struggled while keeping against Anil Kumble, an experience shared by many keepers because of the leg-spinner's pace and bounce, two qualities which differentiated Kumble from the rest. In other words, he had enough to worry about after the series had ended.

Thankfully, his misery didn't continue for too long. The law of averages, a common phrase in cricket, came to his rescue. This happened during India's trip to Zimbabwe for another tri-series in which New Zealand was the third team. After losing to New Zealand in the first match on 26 August 2005, India bulldozed Zimbabwe in the second with Dhoni scoring a quick half-century. In their third match, this time against New Zealand, India returned the compliments with a six-wicket win in which Dhoni scored an unbeaten 37 to facilitate the victory.

Playing against Zimbabwe in the next match, in which the host team managed to put up 250 on the board, India lost their first four wickets for 36 runs. At 91, the fifth wicket went down. But Yuvraj (120) and Dhoni, who ended up with 67 not out, took the team past the finishing line.

In spite of scoring 276, an innings in which Dhoni went back to the pavillion after scoring 11, India lost to New Zealand. At a personal level, however, he could have looked back at the series and said to himself that he hadn't fared too badly. With the ODIs over and Karthik back in the side for the two Test series against Zimbabwe, Dhoni returned to India. India won easily as expected, but eventful days were about to begin—that of the Chappell—Ganguly controversy.

It started off after Ganguly asked for Chappell's advice

on his batting. Known not to mince words, the coach asked Ganguly to quit the team and get back after he had worked on his shortcomings. The statistical fact of this period was that Ganguly's form had actually been terrible. Whether or not his weaknesses could have been eradicated while he was still in the playing eleven was a different issue altogether.

Ganguly's reaction to his coach's statement was both impulsive and self-destructive. He first scored a painstaking century in the first Test at Bulawayo. After registering a three-figure score, he shared the story of his conversation with Chappell on a TV channel. This was followed by a public exhibition of a patch up before the second Test. But the seeds of bitterness and mutual animosity had been sown.

Not much later, an email written by Chappell to the BCCI that contained a vitriolic attack on Ganguly was leaked to the media. This was followed by an exchange of fire between the coach and the player, each a power centre in his own right. The BCCI set up a review committee, which spoke to both Ganguly and Chappell separately. The discussions and meetings led to a superficial patch up. By that time, however, the problem had snowballed into a major controversy. It was a horrible situation which would mess with Ganguly's career as an international cricketer, who had been an inseparable part of the Fab Four, a quartet consisting of Tendulkar, Dravid, VVS Laxman and himself.

While this big drama had hijacked all the limelight, chances of Dhoni's entry into the longer version had increased due to Karthik's poor batting in Zimbabwe. However, he failed with the bat in all the three matches in the Challenger tri-series one-day tournament at Mohali. Soon it was time for the Indo-Sri Lanka ODI series with Sri Lanka coming to

India for an entire tour after eight long years. For Dhoni, this presented with an important opportunity to play against a subcontinental side, which was ranked second in the world with India as many as five steps behind.

In the first match held in Nagpur on 25 October 2005, Tendulkar batted like a king to score 93 as India made 350 for 6. Sri Lanka went down by a massive margin of 152 runs. The second match at Mohali was another one-sided affair after the visitors collapsed for 122 runs. Tendulkar glittered once more with a 69-ball 67. As was the case against Pakistan, India had a 2-0 lead once again. What it couldn't afford to do was to lose the initiative this time. 31 October arrived, bringing with it Dhoni's brightest moment under the sun which turned him into the poster boy of contemporary Indian cricket.

Before the match in Pune, an interesting episode in a discotheque highlights the sort of person Dhoni used to be at the start of his career. Under the strict supervision of Chappell, the Indian team had been sent to a discotheque to unwind for a couple of hours. The news of the team's imminent visit was somehow leaked to the public. As it invariably happens in a cricket-crazy nation like India, a huge crowd had gathered outside the discotheque. However, very few people had managed to find their way inside the place.

When the team arrived, the sound of the discotheque's loud music was drowned by the cacophonic applause of non-cricketing guests. Dhoni was the '183 Man,' the cricketer many were waiting to see for the first time ever. But he was nowhere to be seen. Yuvraj Singh walked in and started jogging across the floor and around the empty tables, coordinating his every step with the beats of the percussion. Sometime later, Dhoni walked in, followed by Harbhajan Singh and Irfan Pathan.

Embarrassed by the loud cheer that accompanied his entry, he took two steps backwards and tried to shield himself behind Pathan. That didn't work, Pathan being another shy person who seemed all ready to run away.

Venugopal Rao melted in the crowd. Murali Karthik chose to sit on a sofa. The focus seesawed between a jogging Yuvraj and a shy Dhoni, who seemed uncertain about dancing. He kept on standing with Pathan, terribly unsure about entering that space where everybody was having a gala time. Eventually, both Pathan and he did. The moment that happened, non-cricketing guests greeted them with more applause. Dhoni, who had discovered some sort of rhythm, and Pathan, who appeared to have invented some strange steps, became uncomfortable once again. To make them feel at ease, the guests went back to their routine once more.

Harbhajan, in the meantime, had chosen to stand next to the DJ and do some bhangra. About half an hour later, Dravid walked in. Chappell, who was already around, was keeping a close eye on his players. Dravid joined Harbhajan and waved to the crowd, which responded in a similar manner—another loud cheer buried the sound of the percussion-heavy DJ remix. Dravid then took to the dance floor. He sure was a person who knew his steps. His sight made Pathan and Dhoni more comfortable. Suddenly, the two of them started dancing freely, with Dhoni swinging his long straight hair left and right with a sense of confidence for the first time since he had entered.

But the moment Dravid left, the scenario was back to square one: in other words, three people together—a shy Dhoni, an equally shy Pathan and an inconspicuous Rao—wondering what they were doing there in the first place. Dravid, who had danced for a brief while before joining Chappell, walked with him into a sound-proof private enclosure with glass doors. That they were having an intense discussion was easy to see. Close to the dance floor, one visibly affluent person pointed towards Chappell inside the enclosure and screamed, 'Will that man drop this boy Dhoni for the match?' Everybody around him started laughing.

The Indian cricket fan is very volatile. When the team is at the top, he deifies the players. But when it is down and out, this same fan can burn the effigies of players. However, after an icon fades away, only wonderful memories remain. Ganguly hadn't declared his career's innings yet. But after he was shunted, all the fantastic memories of his performance had come rushing back to the minds of his fans. Many of them were clearly unhappy with Chappell, and that probably prompted the statement inside the discotheque.

Oblivious of this episode, which had turned into a joke and amused several people in the crowd, Dhoni and Pathan left the floor soon. When an enthusiastic guest pushed him a bit rather deliberately, Dhoni was the one who stood and apologized. Uneasy under the limelight, uncomfortable in a discotheque's surroundings, mild-mannered, a man who seemed to have come to the venue out of curiosity and almost hated his decision: was he the same lad who could be so aggressive when he went out to bat?

He was, and he showed that to the Pune locals during the match that followed. Batting first, Sri Lanka made a respectable 261. The Indian innings was an erratic show. After Tendulkar and Yuvraj fell cheaply, Sehwag (48) and Dravid (63) steadied the ship. Rao made a quick 38, which kept India in the hunt. But his dismissal was followed by that of Dravid and then of Pathan in quick succession. At 180 for 6, India definitely had reasons to worry about.

It was at this stage that a young Suresh Raina joined Dhoni, who was already there at the crease. The two of them remained unbeaten on 39 and 45 respectively to take India home with 26 balls to spare. Initially cautious, but attacking towards the end, Dhoni hit the part-time spinner Russell Arnold for two consecutive sixes to finish the match. What is identified now as his trademark quality was evident in this short but significant innings, which would make him a brilliant finisher, who not only played some peculiar strokes but also had a completely individualistic style of meeting the target.

In spite of Gambhir's and Dravid's centuries, Sri Lanka won the the next outing in Ahmedabad by five wickets. Dhoni was out for a first ball duck. The next match in Rajkot resulted in a seven-wicket win for India. RP Singh picked up five wickets, and Yuvraj scored an unbeaten 79. Dhoni wasn't required to bat. But in the last match at Vadodara, he scored an excellent 80 which played a pivotal role in India's five-wicket win with more than 10 overs left after Sri Lanka had set a target of 245 for India.

India won the seven-match series 6-1 against a much higher-ranked opponent, a proud moment for the team. Sri Lankan coach Tom Moody admitted that 'India...came hard at us from the beginning, some of the things they tried paid off, and from then onwards, they didn't allow us to get into the contest.' Talking to BBC Sport, former Indian opener Chetan Chauhan was critical about sending all-rounders such as Pathan and Jai Prakash up the order at the expense of authentic batsmen such as Suresh Raina and Venugopal Rao, who weren't getting enough opportunities to show their skills. But he agreed that the decision to send Dhoni up the order 'was a good choice.'[14] The reason was backed by facts.

Moody commented on the capability of Indian strokemakers. What he probably should have mentioned was the demoralizing impact of Dhoni, who won the Man of the Series award by scoring 346 runs at an average of 115.33. The Ranchi boy did not do himself any favour by failing with the bat in the following ODI series against South Africa which ended in a 2-2 draw. Karthik, his main rival during that period, had scored just one knock of 50 plus in his last ten Tests. So, he had to make way for Dhoni for whom the big test would begin very soon.

---

[14]'New era for India,' *BBC Sport*, Ayanjit Sen, 1 November 2005. http://news.bbc.co.uk/sport2/hi/cricket/other_international/india/4395994.stm (accessed 18 December 2014).

TOUGH NEW WORLD

EVEN BEFORE COMPLETING his first year in the international arena, Dhoni had turned into the focal point of national attention. Everybody was talking about his ability to gulp down several litres of milk every day, the quantity of which varied according to the journalists' source of information. His long hair and cavalier approach to the game had made him every television broadcaster's delight and won the hearts of numerous women across the country. His hometown's pride, the cricket-loving nation's latest preoccupation, Dhoni had turned into a folk hero even before he had played his first Test match.

Because of his performances in the ODI format, the BCCI had directly offered him a 'B' Grade contract instead of the 'C' Grade which someone as new as him might have expected to get. However, his beginning in the five-day format was unspectacular because of nature's intervention. A cyclone named Baaz ruined Dhoni's first Test against Sri Lanka in Chennai in December 2005. The cricketer in him would have been desperate to get out and play his first match in the longer version, but the first three-and-a-half days disappeared without a ball being bowled. The result of the match—a draw— was a foregone conclusion. How India performed during the remaining time of play was the only factor that deserved some sort of attention.

After the match finally began on the fourth day, all the Indian top-order batsmen except Sehwag batted with exaggerated slowness, including the comeback man, Ganguly. Dhoni was the only Indian batsman who showed the right kind of temperament when he came out to bat on the last day. He made just 30. But the difference lay in the manner in which he got those runs. He faced 54 deliveries, played Murali with ease, and hit six boundaries to add a touch of fluency to the dull nature of the Indian proceedings.

Dhoni took his first ever Test catch that dismissed Avishka Gunawardene. In spite of insufficient scope in the curtailment, the wicketkeeper-batsman might not have been particularly unhappy. During his brief stay at the crease, he had conveyed the message that he could score freely and still be a productive component of India's unit for the five-dayers.

The second Test in Delhi will be remembered in cricketing history as the occasion in which Tendukar went past Sunil Gavaskar's Test record of thirty-four centuries by scoring his thirty-fifth. The new record eclipsed what logically should have been the biggest news of the match—India's victory over Sri Lanka by a margin of 188 runs.

India's score of 290 in the first innings was the consequence of two important knocks—Tendulkar's 109 and Laxman's 69. Dhoni scored just 5 before being cleaned up by Murali's *doosra*[15]. Sri Lanka responded with 230. When India batted, Irfan Pathan, who had been sent out to open the innings, scored a reasonably brisk 93. But the turnaround was engineered by

---

[15]A particular type of delivery bowled by an off-spin bowler.

Dhoni, who changed gears and shifted to the one-day style of batting. He scored an unbeaten 51 off that many deliveries, sharing a century partnership with Yuvraj, who made 77 (not out) but at a much slower rate. If nothing else, Dhoni's half-century showed that the lad had a sharp cricketing brain. He understood what was required of him in that particular situation. And he delivered.

Dravid put Sri Lanka in to bat after declaring the innings at 375 for 6. Sri Lankans failed to put up a fight with Kumble picking up four wickets in the second innings to finish with a ten-wicket haul. Any discussion on Dhoni's performance was eclipsed because of three main reasons—Ganguly's removal from the team for the third Test which led to a huge outcry, Kumble's ten-wicket haul, and of course, Tendulkar's thirty-fifth hundred.

Sehwag was handed over the responsibility of captaining the team in Ahmedabad in the absence of an unwell Dravid. Batting first, India was reduced to 97 for 5. After the dismissal of Mohammed Kaif, who had replaced Dravid, Dhoni joined Laxman, who had dropped anchor and did the opposite of what might have been expected of him in a Test match. He launched a counter-attack that took the Sri Lankan bowlers by complete surprise. By the time he was dismissed for 49, India had reached 183 for 6.

An ESPNcricinfo.com report had a vivid description of his batting, 'Every movement of Dhoni at the crease signalled intent—whether going forward or back, he was decisive in his movement. Whenever bat met ball, it was emphatic, whether in defence or attack. He used his feet but kept his head; he was aggressive but did not take any risks. Sometimes he smashed the ball through empty spaces in the field; at other times, he used the empty space in the air, lofting without inhibition or fear of human intervention.'[16]

On a slow pitch, Indian batsmen crawled on the first day. *The Dawn* in Pakistan observed, 'Wicket-keeper Dhoni was the lone batsman to play shots with freedom against a disciplined Sri Lanka pace-spin combination, hitting seven fours in his 62-ball knock.'[17]

Statistics tend to deceive very often. The memory bank's limited storage capacity makes us susceptible to forgetting the circumstances in which the runs had been scored. When Dhoni went to the crease, he had to make sure that India managed to ensure some self-respect with their first innings score. While Laxman batted patiently, Dhoni launched a fairly successful rescue mission to share an 86-run-partnership with his senior teammate. Pathan, who walked in after Dhoni's dismissal, scored a fine 82 to help India reach 398, after which Harbhajan with his six-wicket haul spun Sri Lanka into abject surrender for 206.

India would eventually inflict a massive defeat on the Lankans and soar to number two in the International Cricket Council (ICC) Test rankings, right below Australia but above England.

Whether or not Dhoni was thinking about his rivalry with Karthik, can be anyone's guess. But Dhoni was reasonably pleased, if not ecstatic, with his performance in his debut

[16]'Laxman leads Indian fightback,' *ESPNcricinfo.com*, Amit Varma, 18 December 2005. http://www.espncricinfo.com/indvsl/content/story/230010.html (accessed 19 December 2014).

[17]'Laxman spares India blushes in final Test,' *The Dawn*, 19 December 2005. http://www.dawn.com/news/170587/laxman-spares-india-s-blushes-in-final-test (accessed 19 December 2014).

series in the longer version of the game. He had collected 149 runs with the bat at an average of 37.25 which included two important knocks of 51 not out and 49. He had taken his first few steps, but he definitely came across as a player who deserved to be in the playing XI with the best in the country.

During the trip to Pakistan in the beginning of 2006, Dhoni's selection was an obvious choice. Ganguly's comeback—said to be backed by the top management—created a void in the opening slot, a task Dravid had to undertake in an atmosphere of bitterness. In a short Test career so far, Dhoni found himself playing in another match in which the weather played the spoilsport—the first Test in Lahore which turned out to be a run feast ending in a draw. But the second Test in Faisalabad would result in a personal landmark for him.

After Pakistan had put up 588 on the board, India's battle to save the follow-on was initially spearheaded by Dravid (103) and Laxman (90). This was followed by a collapse, and the team was struggling at 281 for 5 when Dhoni walked in. For a natural strokeplayer like him, the situation was hardly ideal. Pakistani pacer Shoaib Akhtar was bowling a spell that was, to put it mildly, fearfully hostile. But Dhoni remained unperturbed and did what he did best. He counter-attacked. Akhtar kept on coming at him. Dhoni kept on going after him. Eventually, the pacer was forced to surrender.

Pakistan tried everything they could. But their strategies came to nothing. Leggie Danish Kaneria was sent out of the ground for a massive six. Another six followed. Akhtar had conceded defeat to this belligerent batsman anyway. Before one knew, Dhoni had raced away to 50 from 34 balls. Interestingly, Dhoni slowed down after he completed his half-century. The consequence—he completed his maiden Test century from 93 balls. When the day ended, Dhoni was unbeaten on 116. Pathan who was giving him company, was not out on 49. India had finished the day at 441 for 5, having avoided the follow-on with unexpected ease. Eventually, Dhoni and Pathan shared a 210-run sixth-wicket partnership, India's record for the sixth wicket against Pakistan. Both the batsmen missed individual milestones, with Pathan getting dismissed for 90 and Dhoni getting out for 148. The match ended in a draw.

Dhoni's knock demonstrated that getting intimidated was not a part of his cricket vocabulary. With a classic demonstration of his temperament, he had been able to steer his team out of crisis in his own inimitable style. *Wisden* wrote, 'Dhoni, India's cocky rock star with a neat line in wicketkeeping and outlandish batting, was also peppered around his head and ribs, but it was during this hostility that he announced himself as a Test batsman.'[18]

Dravid said that he hadn't given any instruction to Dhoni about adopting the approach he did. 'I just told him to go out and play his game and do what he knows best. And he attacked brilliantly. It's one of the best counter-attacking innings I have seen in a long, long time. Considering the situation of the game when he came in to play the way he did showed a lot of character, it showed courage and ability.' Apart from his maiden century, the Faisalabad Test had a brief Dhoni episode which will be of interest to trivia collectors. Dhoni bowled his first over in an international match, giving away 13 runs.

---

[18]'India in Pakistan 2005-06,' *Wisden*, Osman Samiuddin. http://www.espncricinfo.com/wisdenalmanack/content/story/290806.html (accessed 19 December 2014).

The third Test in Karachi was lively. This time, Dhoni failed to repeat his magic as India went down by 341 runs to lose the Test series 1-0 in spite of starting out on a great note with Pathan's first-over hat-trick. This was a shocking humiliation, but India needed to recover very fast in order to perform well in the ODI series that followed.

The first ODI at Peshawar went Pakistan's way. Helped by the Duckworth–Lewis method, they put it past India by 7 runs, even after India had put up an imposing total of 328 all out on the board. Tendulkar reached the three-figure mark, Pathan made 65 and Dhoni, a fine 68. Pakistan went past their revised target of 305 with three wickets in hand. In Rawalpindi, India flattened Pakistan by going past 265 with seven wickets in hand. In Lahore, Dhoni lit up the stadium with an astounding display of ruthless batsmanship. Batting first, Pakistan had made 288 for 8. Despite Tendulkar's 95, India had been reduced to 190 for 5 in the thirty-fifth over. That is when Dhoni along with Yuvraj took over.

The two young men shared a 102-run partnership. Those runs were scored in thirteen overs. Yuvraj with his 87-ball 79 not out watched the crackers fly off his partner's bat as he rattled off an unbeaten 72 from 46 balls. With this knock, he went past the 1,000-run mark in the ODIs in twenty-nine innings in thirty-three matches. His average was an extraordinary 50.19, his strike rate an equally amazing 107.44. Although Dravid had taken fewer matches reached the 1,000-run mark, he was just a make-shift keeper. An analysis in *The Hindustan Times* correctly pointed out, 'Among the "genuine" keepers, Dhoni is now the quickest to reach this landmark bettering England's Alec Stewart's record. Stewart had taken thirty-one innings and thirty-four matches to accomplish this feat.'[19]

By achieving the feat, he had gone past Stewart, and significant players such as Sangakkara, Gilchrist and that hugely talented misfit in the Zimbabwe squad of yesteryear—Andy Flower. Within a short period, he had showed why he deserved all the adulation he got.

More was on the way in the Indo-Pak series. In the Multan tie, Dhoni wasn't required to bat. In the fifth match in Karachi, Pakistan again set a reasonably daunting target by scoring 286 for 8. What followed there was a Yuvraj–Dhoni encore. The stylish left-hander scored a hundred, while Dhoni made an unbeaten 77 from 56 balls with four sixes and six fours. Pakistani bowlers were treated with disdain as India won by eight wickets to win the series 4-1. Yuvraj became the Man of the Series, but Dhoni, who had been dismissed just once, averaged 219 which included three half centuries.

Speaking to the PTI after the series ended, Pakistan skipper Inzamam-ul-Haq said that Dhoni 'is safe behind the wickets and can be compared with Adam Gilchrist though the Australian has proved himself as the best after years in the game.'[20] Slowly but surely, the Indian wicketkeeper-batsman was turning into a force to reckon with. In journalistic language, he was the latest breaking news for everyone who was in love with the game.

Having burst into the national scene from nowhere, this

---

[19]'A world record for MS Dhoni', *The Hindustan Times*, 14 February 2006. http://www.hindustantimes.com/news-feed/archives/a-world-record-for-ms-dhoni/article1-65763.aspx (accessed 19 December 2014).
[20]'Dhoni can be compared with Gilchrist: Inzamam,' *The Hindu*, 22 February 2006. http://www.thehindu.com/todays-paper/tp-sports/dhoni-can-be-compared-with-gilchrist-inzamam/article3181738.ece (accessed 19 December 2014).

youngster's beginning had been so remarkable that it seemed that he would define the future of Indian cricket. Soon, the England team came visiting India under the captaincy of Andrew Flintoff. The three-match Test series produced a 1-1 result, but the Englishmen were definitely the happier lot considering they had drawn a Test series with India at the latter's home.

In Nagpur, the venue of the first Test that began on 1 March 2006, everybody was hoping that England would lose badly because of issues pertaining to withdrawals and injuries. But nothing of the sort happened. In the Mohali Test, India sailed to a victory by nine wickets. But in Mumbai, fortunes changed. This time, India was at the receiving end. Responding to England's score of 400, Dhoni and the lower order gave a semblance of dignity to the Indian score. Dravid had scored a 50, but there was hardly anything else worth talking about until Dhoni joined Pathan at the crease.

Dhoni eventually went on to score 64, the highest in the innings and his personal highest in the series. More than the amount of runs that he scored, it was how he scored that was noticeable. He kept on scoring in singles, got hit on the head by a Flintoff bouncer on the way, and was dismissed by a wrong decision. A throw from James Anderson hit the stumps when he was scampering for a single, catching him out of crease. The ground umpire Darrell Hair had referred the run-out appeal to the third umpire K Hariharan. Replays showed that the bails had not been dislodged when Dhoni made it to the crease. In a report with a dramatic headline 'Was Dhoni out?' Rediff.com said, 'Hariharan is said to have watched the replay six times, but to the utter surprise of many, including England's former captains David Gower and Michael

Atherton, ruled Dhoni out.'[21] The wicketkeeper-batsman had been shortchanged by a shocking verdict. Another one which led to a lot of drama was to follow soon.

England, who had a 121-run lead in the first innings, was all out for 191 in the second. India's target of 312 when they batted was, to use a worn out commentating cliche, 'gettable'. What followed was a performance few would have expected. The batsmen were sent packing for 100 with Dhoni scoring 5. Now it was time for the one-dayers. India had to prove that the bizarre batting performance in the second innings in Mumbai was like a very bad day at office whose memory had been left far behind.

India would go on to bulldoze England 5-1 in a one-sided ODI series. Presented with many opportunities during this period, Dhoni's one significant performance against England was an assault on their bowlers in Jamshedpur. The innings of 96 was a standout show, but the English team managed to pull off a consolation win. *Indian Express* suggested that a cricket fan could have blamed it on the 'Jamshedpur jinx' since the home team had lost seven out of the nine matches they had played at the Keenan Stadium.[22]

The distinguishing fact of this Dhoni innings was that he had played as an opener and watched wickets tumble at the other end until the team was reduced to 79 for 5. In came Romesh Powar, who hit the only fifty of his career and shared an important partnership with Dhoni until the latter got out

---

[21]'Was Dhoni out?,' *Rediff.com*, 20 March 2006. http://www.rediff.com/cricket/2006/mar/20dhoni.htm (accessed 19 December 2014).
[22]'India fail to break the Jamshedpur jinx,' *Indian Express*, Maneesh Kumar, 12 April 2006. http://www.indiaexpress.com/news/sports/cricket/20060412-4.html (accessed 19 December 2014).

for 96 with the score at 186. The Indian tail didn't wag for long and the innings folded up for 223, which England— propelled by their skipper Andrew Strauss—overtook with ease.

Strauss was generous while complimenting Dhoni. 'Right through this series, Dhoni has shown how versatile he is as a batsman. He can come in and spank the ball if the situation so demands, or he can come up the order and knock it around like he did today. It was a very good knock.' What this performance also showed was that Dhoni was getting used to the role of playing the saviour. India were in deep trouble. He soaked in the pressure and delivered a masterclass. He couldn't get to a personal landmark of a three-figure mark. His heroics could not save the day for India. But he had led the way, once again.

By now, Dhoni had become an important member of the Indian ODI side. His debut against Bangladesh in which he had scored 12 runs at an average of 9.50 had turned into an irrelevant statistic. When Pakistan had come down to India in the 2000-05 season, he had added 261 runs to his tally, averaging 43.50, largely because of his extraordinary knock of 148. He hadn't done much in the tri-series featuring Sri Lanka, the West Indies and India thereafter, managing to score only 72 runs at an average of 24. In the tri-series against New Zealand and Zimbabwe, he had scored 177 runs at an average of 57.66.

When the Sri Lankans had come down to India, he sparkled with the bat to pile up 346 runs with a 183 not out, at his highest at an average of 115.33. If he had delivered one dismal performance, it was against the South Africans in the drawn series towards the end of 2005. Against Pakistan in early 2006, he averaged a mind-boggling 219. Against England, the contribution of a handful of runs during the two occasions he had remained not out—two innings of 20 and 38 and one big knock of 96—had ensured a highly respectable average of 59. After the victory over the Englishmen, India climbed to the number three spot in the ICC ODI rankings. For Dhoni as an individual, the national team he played for and the coach–captain duo of Chappell and Dravid, everything seemed fine.

The DLF Cup in April 2006 was a two-match series between arch-rivals India and Pakistan. The latter won the first tie, but India bounced back in the second with a 51-run win. Apart from Sehwag's rollicking 73 and Dravid's composed 92, Dhoni scored an unusually sedate 59 to take India to a respectable score of 269 for 5. Pakistan were all out for 218.

Having tied the series 1-1, it was time to proceed to the Caribbean. Dhoni on his part enjoyed a brief moment under the spotlight by occupying the number one position in ICC ODI rankings in the first week of April 2006. He replaced Ricky Ponting and hung on to the position for a couple of weeks after which he was overtaken by Adam Gilchrist. At that time, his career statistics made for awesome reading. He had played in 42 matches, averaged 52.76 with a couple of hundreds and eight fifties. His strike rate of 103 was nothing short of intimidating. Apart from the honour itself, he had journeyed to the top and now knew how it felt when one reached the number one spot in the world.

One of the most frequently used phrases in cricket is that the game is a great leveller. Dhoni would experience it very soon. His ODI show in the West Indies tour was a dismal one. He managed to score 95 runs in five matches, and his string of scores—18, 2, 15, 46 not out, 14—made for disappointing reading. The Test series that followed diminished the bitter memories of the loss in the ODIs. For the first time since 1971, India won a series against the West Indies in the latter's home soil 1-0. But, the fact of the matter was that the West Indies had been thoroughly outplayed.

Dhoni had a very mediocre series, scoring 168 at an average of 24. But he did play a spectacular knock in the second innings at St Johns, Antigua. Batting first, India scored 241. West Indies responded with 371. In the second innings, opener Wasim Jaffer scored 212, a pivotal double ton which was crucial in taking the Indian score to 512 for 6 declared. Batting freely, Dhoni, who came in to bat at number seven, raced away to 69 from 52 balls in 51 minutes. He hit six sixes out of which three came off consecutive deliveries against the gentle spin of Dave Mohammed.

Then, he hit another shot. The aim was the same—clearing the boundary. But Darren Ganga caught the ball right on the edge of the mid-wicket boundary. In spite of consultations with the third umpire Billy Doctrove, none of the TV replays could deliver a conclusive judgment on whether or not Ganga had caught a travelling aerial ball within the legally specified limits. At this point in time, it was disturbing to see how Lara responded. The West Indian legend not only threw tantrums, but got so furious at the umpires that he showed them the finger and snatched the ball from them.

A witness to the entire farce, Dhoni took the initiative and decided to return to the pavilion. In a front-page article, *The Telegraph* wrote, 'After 15 minutes of high drama and utter confusion, the Indian wicketkeeper-batsman was officially given out only after returning to the dressing room. Never before had Test cricket witnessed such a bizarre incident.' It also mentioned what the Indian player had to say. 'Brian Lara came to me and said he was taking charge of his players and whatever they say was going to be the truth and "I think you should walk off". Dhoni later said. "I was walking off the field when I had eye contact with the umpires and decided to stay put."[23]

The incident didn't snowball into a never-ending controversy. But no genuine cricket lover was pleased with what had happened either.

The second Test at St Lucia was a washout. The third Test at St Kitts ended in another draw, but the fourth one at Kingston gave India what they had been threatening to get all along—a richly-deserved win. In a low-scoring match dominated by the bowlers, India won by 49 runs.

The verdict was hugely encouraging, but dull news was in store. The three-match ODI series ended against Sri Lanka with only 11 runs being scored in the first match before the rains played the spoilsport. The next two matches were washouts. Playing in the DLF Cup, a tri-series tournament featuring the West Indies and Australia, India fared badly. Dhoni scored 43 runs in three innings with a highest of 23. After that, it was time for the ICC Champions Trophy with India playing host.

India's performance in the tournament simply added to their list of flop shows. A four-wicket win against England in Jaipur was followed by three-wicket loss against the West Indies in Ahmedabad. Dhoni scored a reasonably calm 51 from 65 balls. But that was not enough as the tourists won the match with two balls to spare. Confronting a must-win scenario

---

[23]'Play crosses the line—Dispute over Dhoni "dismissal" prompts Lara to snatch ball from umpire; declaration saves the day,' *The Telegraph*, 7 June 2006. http://www.telegraphindia.com/1060607/asp/frontpage/story_6321217.asp (accessed 21 December 2014).

against the Australians in their Mohali encounter, India hardly posed any challenge as the latter cruised to a six-wicket win. Dhoni made a quickfire 28 from 23 balls when India set a target of 249 for 8. In the end, the Australians went past that target with 26 balls remaining.

India's misery didn't end there. Playing against the South Africans in the latter's homeground towards the end of 2006, the team was demolished by 4-0. Dhoni scored 139 runs in the four outings at an average of 34.75, which included a swashbuckling knock of 55 from 48 balls in Cape Town. His form hadn't dipped to a horrifying low, but the team was down and out. The World Cup was just around the corner. This was not the sort of record any cricketing nation would have aspired for.

Would India face a similar verdict while playing the Test matches against a team on a winning streak at their home turf? Speculations grounded in reality would have led to the same conclusion. They would. What nobody would have predicted is the difference the inclusion of former skipper, Ganguly, would make, since it was his gritty unbeaten half century in the first innings which provided the momentum for an Indian win by 123 runs in the first Test at Johannesburg.

At Durban, they were thrashed by 174 runs. Chasing a target of 354 runs in the second innings, the batsmen struggled against a hostile pace attack in a manner which was a pathetic sight for every fan of Indian cricket. Dhoni scored 34 and 47 in the two innings. That was hardly disappointing, yet irrelevant in the context of the outcome. In the third Test at Cape Town, he was compelled to sit out because of injury to his fingers and a chest infection. Dinesh Karthik replaced him and the South Africans won.

At the ninth ICC World Cup being hosted by the West Indies in March, 2007, India needed to perform. For that to happen, the team needed to gain some momentum. Inspirational performances had to come from somewhere. Demoralized like the players themselves, Indian cricket fans had already started mulling over that one important question. How will India fare at the World Cup?

The year 2007 started on a promising note. West Indies came to India. They were beaten 3-1. Sri Lankans who toured thereafter, lost 2-1. The biggest news was that Ganguly made a surprising comeback, adding a twist to the narrative which hardly anybody would have anticipated.

In the first ODI at Nagpur, India piled up 338 for 3. The former skipper made a crucial 98 that anchored the innings till he got out. Dhoni made a stupendous return to form. Not only did he score 62 from 42 balls—the good old Dhoni show was back in town—but he also shared a whirlwind partnership of 119 runs with Dravid. West Indies fought hard, but they lost by 14 runs.

India put it past the West Indies in a low-scoring second ODI at Cuttack. After losing the Chennai tie, Dhoni who had been rested for the match returned in Vadodara and smashed an unbeaten 40 from 20 balls. The description of Dhoni's whirlwind knock in ESPNCricinfo suggested the hint of a smile on the writer's face, 'Tendulkar, on 67 when Dhoni walked in, did not seem to realistically think he would make it to three figures, and was simply content turning the strike over and letting Dhoni loose on the bowlers. Dhoni certainly didn't mind, and proceeded to whip the bowlers to all parts. Long-off, long-on, midwicket, the corporate office of Indian Petrochemicals Corporation Limited just outside the ground—nothing was spared as the ball disappeared to all parts.'[24]

Tendulkar did get a superb century though, as India demolished the clueless Windies. The 'Little Master' went on to become the Man of the Series, but Dhoni scored 108 runs in three matches while being dismissed just once. His strike rate of 133.33 was perfect for a Twenty20 match, a format which was destined to become a significant aspect of his career—both as a brilliant finisher and a leader of men.

The first India–Sri Lanka match in the next home series ended without a result. But the Lankans, who won the second tie by 5 runs in Rajkot, took a 1-0 lead. Dhoni's 68-ball 48 was clearly the outcome of his decision to hang on till the end which didn't materialize. Having turned into the Indian icon of flamboyant batting resulted in a separate discussion on his strike rate.

At Margao, the visitors set a target of 230 for 8. It seemed easily achievable, until India batted, only to be reduced to 94 for 4. But Dhoni and Dravid came together to chaperon India to the target by sharing a 133-run partnership. Dravid led while the man who would become 'Captain Cool' was content to play the second fiddle for most part of the partnership.

Eventually, Dhoni was the one who remained not out on 67 as India won after the initial jitters in a tricky chase. 'Dhoni has a mature head. He plays according to the situation. If we need a quick-fire innings, he plays that; and if we need a controlled innings, he plays that,' Dravid said after India

---

[24]'A batting line-up to die for,' Cricinfo, Anand Vasu, 31 January 2007. http://m.espncricinfo.com/indvwi/content/story/278350.html (accessed 21 December 2014).

posted a five-wicket win. Speaking of the veteran and the young man in the same breath, the famously sporting Lankan skipper Jayawardene admitted that the manner in which the two of them batted and controlled the Indian innings won the match for the home team. India's easy win in the last match in which Dhoni wasn't required to bat meant that he had batted twice in the series to end up with a 100-plus average two times on the trot.

Having started out on a promising note, Dhoni was now battle-ready for his first ICC World Cup in the West Indies. India had enjoyed some successes in their home soil, but overall indications in the previous twelve months did little to suggest that the team would put up a fight for the trophy. However, the mood across the country was predictably optimistic. Sections of the media went all out to resurrect memories of the highly improbable Indian win in 1983. The viewer was frequently reminded that Ganguly's men needed just one win to bring the trophy home in the previous edition of the tournament. Stories of India's famous exploits were repeatedly telecast with ones of losses concealed from public view. Several newspapers carried articles on India's major World Cup wins. Relegated to the sidelines were ones of humiliating losses. That the national team had won the last two ODI series before the World Cup became a pivotal topic of discussion very often. Because of the carefully orchestrated build-up, the average cricket follower should have been excused for believing that India stood a chance. A positive chance.

Once in the West Indies, reality stung in the first match itself. Prone to losing their first outing at the World Cup— India had a dubious record of going down five out of eight times earlier India met Bangladesh. The minnows thrashed the favourites by five wickets with Dhoni scoring a duck. After this shocking humiliation, India needed a miracle to proceed to the critical Super Eight stage. That they would thrash Bermuda, possibly the worst team to have played in the ODIs ever, was a given. They also had to beat Sri Lanka in their match by a good-enough margin. If they lost to Sri Lanka, they had to expect that Bermuda would beat Bangladesh which was a slightly unprobable scenario.

The India–Bermuda tie was a bit of a joke. As if keen to prove that they had been distinctly lucky to be there in the first place, Bermuda allowed India to score 413 for 5. Bermuda replied with 156, leading to an easy Indian victory by 257 runs, the biggest margin of win till then. With one verdict in their favour—against the easiest competitor India could have asked for—23 March was to be a potentially fate-deciding day for the team.

Sri Lanka, a seriously strong opposition, had already qualified for the Super Eight stage. India had not. Having erred by choosing to bat first against Bangladesh, Dravid sent the opposition in to bat this time. The Lankans were restricted to 254 for 6, the target of 255 thus set. The target was far from intimidating for a supposedly strong Indian batting line-up.

Watching India respond was a heart-breaking experience. Tendulkar failed. So did Ganguly. Yuvraj got run out. Sehwag fell two short of fifty. Fighting a lonely battle, Dravid watched a procession at the other end. Dhoni was trapped leg before wicket by Muttiah Muralitharan. It was a first-ball duck. He walked without waiting for the bowler to appeal and the umpire raising his finger. In hindsight, he should not have done that. But the decision to leave the pitch might have simply been an impulsive one; or maybe, he was trying to avoid the inevitable that would have followed a few seconds later. When the last wicket of tailender Munaf Patel fell, the total stood at 185. Sri Lanka had won easily by 69 runs.

India waited for two days for the result of the Bermuda-Bangladesh tie. As expected, Bermuda did not cast any spell on their far superior rivals. After the result, India's World Cup journey came to an end. The cacophonic hype that had preceded the trip to the Caribbean had been silenced. Dhoni had a forgettable tournament in which his string of scores read 0, 29, 0. However, the statistics of his performance had become a minor fact as the focus shifted to the two navigators, Dravid and Chappell.

In a media interaction, Dravid spoke as candidly as he could have. When asked whether he realized the enormity of the loss, the beleaguered skipper admitted, 'No one realizes the enormity more than the players. I know you all feel bad and people back home will feel bad, but no one feels as bad as the players themselves. A lot of our dreams and hopes were based around this competition, the biggest one-day event.' He added that, as the team leader, the responsibility for the failure was his. 'I am not shirking it, I am the first one to stand up and take responsibility. We didn't do well, and I take full responsibility for us not progressing to the next stage. We were not up to scratch, and we didn't deserve to go through to the next stage.'

If Dhoni escaped being under the spotlight, it was largely because the media's focus on Dravid and Chappell had turned him into just another player in a team sport. The most controversial coach in the history of Indian cricket—and in fact, any form of team sport played in the country, Chappell declared his innings. His statement read, 'Today I informed the president of the BCCI that I would not seek an extension to my contract to coach the Indian cricket team for family and personal reasons.'

While Kumble announced his retirement after the World Cup no-show, Dravid's position, while shaky, didn't appear to be under immediate threat. BCCI Secretary Niranjan Shah shared his view with Rediff.com, 'First of all, Dravid isn't the only person responsible for India's pathetic performance in the World Cup. If India had made it to the Super Eights everyone would have praised his captaincy. But because we didn't, people are now talking about finding a replacement for him. In my personal opinion, and I'm saying this not as the BCCI secretary but as a cricket lover, we should continue with Dravid at the helm of Team India. This is my personal view only, let me emphasise.'[25] In a PTI report carried by ibnlive.com, he made a significant addition, 'I feel another youngster can be groomed under him to take over at a later stage.'[26]

When Shah had spoken about the possibility of grooming a youngster, did he have somebody in mind? Those who had latched on to Shah's statement would have mulled over these questions, although one look at the Indian line-up did suggest that the chosen one should be a young lad, who could harness his mental resources properly and play according to situational needs by abandoning, modifying or adhering to his natural style of play. The only name that came to mind

[25]'Board secretary Shah backs Dravid,' *Rediff.com*, Haresh Pandya, 2 April 2007. http://www.rediff.com/wc2007/2007/apr/02inter.htm (accessed 21 December 2014).
[26]Ibid.

was of a player who had showcased his skills and calmness in the shorter version in particular and also become a good-enough wicketkeeper at the international level.

ASCENSION AND GLORY

INDIAN CRICKET HAS two types of fans. The first among them is the dignified supporter, who exults when India wins and feels low when the opposite happens. At the same time, this person understands that a cricketer goes through ups and downs and also that winning and losing are part of the game. The second kind is the vulgar fan. India being a nation of 1.2 billion people has many fans of this detestable variety. Those who are mild among them restrict themselves to hurling abuses when a batsman gets out for cheap, or the opposition's batsmen plunder the bowling and, of course, when the team loses a match. Others show their destructive streak, which is far worse.

Because of larger issues such as Chappell's resignation and the failures of the veterans to perform in India's ICC World Cup campaign, Dhoni had been reduced to a footnote in the national media. In Ranchi, however, local hooligans decided to make a statement of disgust by attacking his under-construction house after he fell for a duck against Bangladesh. Such was the nature of vandalism that a wall was demolished. After India lost to Sri Lanka with Dhoni scoring a duck again, special armed security personnel had to be deployed at his Shyamali colony residence and also at his own house which was under construction at that time.

What happened after the World Cup fiasco was vandalism at its worst. But, Indian cricket had been marred by such episodes in the past, although Dhoni and his family had experienced it for the first time ever. Outside Ranchi, it was quickly forgotten as more cricketing action followed. A few weeks after their shameful exit from the World Cup, India went on a tour of Bangladesh. With Chappell having gone, former India skipper and all-rounder Ravi Shastri was appointed as the cricket manager. Bangladesh had shocked India in the ICC World Cup, the memories of which hadn't faded away. In spite of the objective reality that India were a far superior side, the fear of surprising failures haunted people's minds.

At Mirpur, history threatened to repeat itself. In a rain-curtailed match, Bangladesh, who batted first, put up a more than respectable score of 250 for 7. By the time India had reached 114, five batsmen had been dismissed. Another 107 were needed from 113 balls, and Dhoni was at the crease with Karthik. Having been sent in to bat at the fall of the first wicket, he scored a Man-of-the-Match-winning innings of 91 not out and shared an unbeaten century stand with Karthik to guide the team to a win.

What was important about this match was not the number of runs Dhoni scored, but the manner in which he got them. When he was batting on 39, he started suffering from cramps because of the hot and humid weather. Yuvraj Singh walked in as the runner and, what's more, Bangladesh bowlers started bowling away from him to capitalize on his restricted feet movement. Dhoni began dealing in singles and twos, hit only seven boundaries, and ensured that the team didn't have to press the panic button by remaining unbeaten.

After the match was over, Dravid acknowledged, 'He

(Dhoni) does not play in just one fashion. He has got the ability to change gears, to change the tempo of the game, play according to the situation and that's a fantastic gift to have at such a young age.' In his own quiet and unassuming manner, this young man had led from the front, if the word 'leading' were to imply that he had to be on the field for almost the entire day. Cramps affected him, but he hung on nevertheless. He did not try his trademark shots. Helped by Karthik, he took his team out of trouble and erased the memory of a recent defeat at the World Cup which had catalysed the exit of his team in the preliminary stage itself.

From thereon, India were on a roll. They won the second match with ease before rains came visiting in the third tie and also in the drawn first Test. In the second Test, they demolished Bangladesh by an innings and 239 runs. After piling up 610 for 3 with the top four batsmen scoring centuries, Bangladesh was dismissed twice and the match came to an end in less than three days. Dhoni scored an unbeaten 51, which didn't do much apart from adding more runs to the margin of defeat.

Soon, the second Afro-Asia Cup followed. Contested between two teams consisting of players from various major cricket-playing nations in Africa and Asia, few cricket lovers took the tournament seriously, including die-hard cricket fans in India. Asia XI won without significant resistance. Dhoni, who hadn't managed to make much of an impact in the first two ICC-sanctioned ODIs, performed brilliantly in the third. He mauled the opposition's attack to score an unbeaten 139, and also shared a 218-run partnership with his skipper, the Sri Lankan batting maestro Mahela Jayawardene, a world record for the sixth wicket. Dhoni's third century was another classic example of his passion for seeing his team through to a victory. Once set, he tried really hard not to give his wicket away cheaply. Belligerence was his natural quality and so was determination. As years went by, he would temper and control his strokemaking more often as he took on the responsibility of winning matches as the skipper of a successful squad.

Top Indian cricketers, it is often misconstrued, make a lot of money and enjoy a great life. The fact is partly untrue. They make a lot of money, but don't know how to spend it because of their maddening schedules. Without getting any significant breathing space, Dhoni accompanied the Indian team to the United Kingdom to play ODIs first. India beat South Africa, a contest for the Future Cup by a margin of 2-1 at Belfast. This was followed by a one-off tie against Scotland at Glasgow which India won easily by seven wickets. Dhoni wasn't required to bat.

This was followed by the real big thing—a three Test series against the Englishmen. India's record on English soil hadn't been great, the team having won for the last time under Kapil Dev's captaincy way back in 1986. The initial signs in this series seemed to suggest that India was on the backfoot. Rains came to their rescue on the last day, and once again, Dhoni came to the team when it mattered.

Asked to chase down 380 runs to win the match, India had a tough first Test at Lord's as the ball swung in typically English conditions. Dhoni had made a duck in the first innings, and his second innings of 76 not out in the second wasn't a treat to watch either. He looked shaky, had his share of luck when a clear lbw appeal against him was turned down by umpire Steve Bucknor, but managed to guide the team to the safety of a draw. For India, the fact that only fifty-five overs were bowled in the final day proved to be a lucky charm, the man giving company to Dhoni being the last batsman, S Sreesanth. But had not the boy from Ranchi hung on till the last ball that was bowled, the team would have crashed to a defeat in the first match itself. Dravid—while saying that India had 'got out of jail'—praised Dhoni's effort once again. The relieved wicketkeeper-batsman said that the verdict seemed almost 'like a win' after India seemed down and out. He didn't highlight his match-saving performance, a personality trait cricket lovers would observe time and again in future.

India registered a fantastic win in the second Test, their 200th Test overseas. Dhoni failed with the bat, but he would receive the biggest news of his cricketing career very soon. For his fine batting, reasonably good wicketkeeping and, above all, an unflappable temperament, he was not only named the deputy to Dravid for the ODI team but also made the captain of the forthcoming inaugural World Twenty20 tournament in South Africa. Slowly, but surely, Indian cricket was experiencing the first tremors of a quiet revolution.

With a 1-0 lead and a chance to win the Pataudi Trophy, Dravid's men went into the third Test and scored a huge 664 in their first innings. In spite of England conceding a huge lead, Dravid decided not to enforce a follow on and was satisfied with a draw. Kumble finally got to his first hundred, while Dhoni, who batted under no pressure in the first innings, batted at his fluent best, scoring an 81-ball 92 inclusive of four sixes and nine fours. One month later, Dravid stepped down as captain.

After winning such an important Test series in England, India played a one-off ODI against Scotland. And won. What followed was a seven-ODI Natwest Series against England. Dhoni hardly excelled with the bat in the first six matches, his highest being a meagre 35 in the sixth outing. As a keeper, however, he was responsible for a record-making six dismissals in the fifth match—that included five catches and one stumping. Before the last match, the series was tantalisingly tied at 3-3. In the decider at the Lord's, India crumbled for 187. Dhoni made a sedate 72-ball 50, his highest. England cruised to a win with seven wickets in hand, a disappointing climax of a seemingly unending tour for the Indian team. Dhoni and many others had no break after the end of this exhausting experience. The first World Twenty20 was on its way.

Although Twenty20 as a format has become increasingly popular since, back then the Indian team had played just one international match before going to South Africa. In fact, that one-off tie was against the hosts of World Twenty20 which the Sehwag-led Indian outfit had won by six wickets. Dhoni, on his part, had faced just two balls before being dismissed without scoring. The World Twenty20 squad had some significant changes. Three seniors had opted out, all of them batsmen—Rahul Dravid, Sachin Tendulkar and Sourav Ganguly. The occasion marked the return of Sehwag, Irfan Pathan and Harbhajan Singh, who had been kept out of the Test and ODI squads earlier. Yuvraj Singh was made the vice captain, and there was a feeling that having made his debut before Dhoni, he wasn't exactly happy with the decision. The team also had two newcomers in medium pacer—Joginder Sharma and Yusuf Pathan. Yusuf, Irfan's elder brother, bowled a few overs of spin and had also developed a reputation for hitting the ball really hard and high.

So, South Africa it was, with Dhoni, whose experience in leadership had nothing to write home about, leading a squad which had very little exposure to the shortest version of the game. Years later, in 2011, Sharad Pawar, who was the president of the BCCI in 2007, made an interesting revelation about Dhoni's selection as the skipper. Speaking at a function to felicitate Tendulkar's revered coach Ramakant Achrekar, Pawar shared, 'In August 2007, Rahul Dravid was the captain of the Indian cricket team playing in England. He expressed his willingness to step down. When I asked Rahul to recommend his successor, he said Sachin can be a good captain.'

Because of Dravid's suggestion, Pawar invited Sachin for a discussion. It was Sachin, he said, who recommended MS Dhoni's name as the captain because Sachin thought he is capable of handling the pressure of captaincy better. The former BCCI President admitted, 'I was surprised with Sachin's recommendation, but Dhoni's name was discussed and finalised at a meeting held to select the team for the first Twenty20 World Cup in South Africa in September 2007. Now we all know Sachin's recommendation was so right because it led us to several victories including the Twenty20 World Cup and ICC World Cup triumphs.' Back then, the Little Master had seen the signs.

Twenty-six years is quite young for someone who is leading a major national squad. During a media interaction, he proudly spoke about himself as a Jharkhand lad: 'It's (Jharkhand) a small state where the infrastructure isn't great for cricket. Five years ago, nobody would have ever thought that someone from the state would play for India. Now, if I look back, I am excited for the job.' The Dhoni, who spoke then, was nowhere as articulate as we see now; yet, he had graduated since his Kharagpur days when he had admitted after a cricket match that he didn't know how to talk. From being a player who couldn't express himself after winning a Man of the Match award in Kharagpur to one who addressed a press conference as the Indian captain, Dhoni's evolving narrative appeared to be straight out of the pages of a novel with a series of pleasant dreams.

The World Twenty20 in 2007 made a huge contribution to the cause of the format, which most experts believed would dilute and ultimately destroy the character of the sport. Interestingly, the BCCI had resisted the concept of a world championship for the longest period and Pawar had voted against it. But the inaugural edition showed that the format, which was essentially a batsman's game dominated by uninhibited strokeplay, attracted numerous viewers the world over. Cynicism about its potential amongst serious watchers of the longer version of the game had to make way for the new reality of modern times. It wouldn't be long before national boards started their domestic Twenty20 tournaments like the Indian Premier League and the Big Bash League in Australia as the format became increasingly popular.

In the first edition of the World Twenty20, the teams had been divided into four groups in the preliminary stages. India had been clubbed together in the Group D with Pakistan and Scotland. According to the specified rules the top two teams of each group advanced to the Super Eight stage. The opener, a Group A match between South Africa and the West Indies, gave an excellent idea of what this format was all about. The West Indies piled up a mind-blowing 205 for 6 from their 20 overs, the score anchored by Chris Gayle's century. But then came the twist. Instead of going down meekly, the South Africans went past the target with 14 balls to spare and 8 wickets in hand. Herschelle Gibbs did his own version of Gayle by making an unbeaten 90 from 55 balls, and the end result seemed to guarantee that the format would prove to be the bowler's graveyard in the long run. The match was followed by two strange results in the subsequent days. Zimbabwe went past limited overs cricket champions Australia first, and then Bangladesh ousted the West Indies from the tournament.

India were going through worrying times. Pakistan defeated Scotland by 51 runs, while the tie between Dhoni's men and Scotland was washed out. In a three-team group, the India–Pakistan result became a battle for survival for the former. To make things worse, Dravid announced in Bangalore that he was resigning from the captaincy of both the Test and ODI teams. No matter what the provocation might have been, nobody can question that Dravid's timing was bad. Without having stepped into the field as a captain for the first time ever, Dhoni had to handle the tough job of talking to his team and persuading them to retain their composure. A few days after Dravid's resignation, Dhoni would be made the captain of the Indian ODI team as well.

In order to prove that he could control a game amidst adversities was Dhoni's first target. The first match turned out to be a classic clash. Pakistan's bowling led by Mohammad Asif reduced India to 36 for 4, a condition from which the team couldn't quite recover despite a valiant attempt to rebuild the innings by a young Robin Uthappa (50) and Dhoni (33). The team finished at 141 for 9, certainly not the sort of target Dhoni would have liked to set, despite the bowling-friendly conditions.

Pakistan didn't respond extraordinarily either. Shoaib Malik was the fifth batsman to be dismissed at 87, and they were eventually left with a target of 37 runs off 14 deliveries. India appeared to have the match in its pocket, but the penultimate over in which Agarkar went for 17 facilitated a turnaround. In the final Sreesanth over, the scores were tied with two more balls left to be bowled. Skipper Misbah-ul-Haq missed the fifth delivery. In the last, he was run out after scoring 53 from 35 deliveries. That resulted in a 'bowl-out' situation to decide the winner.

Indians knew about the bowl-out, in which players from both sides have to roll their arms over and hit the stumps. The Pakistanis were unaware of the rule, unlike the Indians who had been preparing to deal with such a possibility during practice sessions. Hence, Indians sent those who had been hitting the stumps more frequently than the others. Sehwag, Harbhajan and Uthappa were deadly accurate, while Yasir Arafat, Umar Gul and Shahid Afridi missed by a fair distance as India wriggled their way out of the crisis by winning the match to reach the Super Eight stage.

Malik was naturally unhappy after the match ended. 'When the match ended in a tie, only then we came to know that this [bowl-out] would happen. I just told my bowlers not to take pressure and try and hit the wickets but they were not successful.' In spite of winning the match, Dhoni didn't abstain from criticising the rule either. 'I won't want to see a cricket match decided on a bowl-out. The team plays so hard to get a result and it should always be decided on the field.' But the bottom line was that the team had been able to pull it off, Dhoni's master-stroke being his introduction of a non-bowler like Uthappa who, he must have observed, could hit the stumps accurately during practice sessions.

Now, the Indian team had to move on. In the Super Eight stage, they were clubbed together in the same group as New Zealand, England and South Africa. In the first match, they experienced a reversal when the bespectacled Black Cap spinner Daniel Vettori spun them out of the game after Sehwag and Gambhir had given a great opening stand when India responded to their total of 190. Dhoni's 24 was of very little use.

India's second fixture against England will be best remembered for the heroics of Yuvraj, who hit Stuart Broad for six sixes in an over. Aided by a 136-run opening partnership shared by Sehwag and Gambhir, India reached 218 for 4. England tried hard, but fell short by 18 runs. Having watched Yuvraj in such form from the other end, Dhoni, who hadn't hit a single four in his unbeaten 10, said later that he had been recently asked whether Yuvraj was in the team primarily for his bowling ability. 'I don't think I have to answer that question now,' he said, happy that a small hurdle had been crossed.

In the final Super Eight match in Durban, South Africa, who had been the only unbeaten team in the tournament so far, needed only 126 to qualify for the semis. For the Indians, a score of 61 for 4 at one stage wasn't a great situation to be in. But Rohit Sharma (50) and Dhoni (45) carried the team to 153 for 5. Unsure of whether to go for a win or simply meet their target, South Africa messed it up and finished at 116 for 9. On that day, another new talent emerged on the Indian cricket scene—Rohit Sharma, whose brilliant batting and fielding won him the Man of the Match award. 'I don't think many people expected us to defend that score,' said Dhoni, after India had pulled off that crucial win. He was right. But then, the team under his leadership had fought hard as a united eleven, who meant business on the field.

Then came the semis in which India took on Australia. Batting first, India scored 188 for 5, thanks to one quick innings of Uthappa (34), and two super quick ones from Yuvraj

(70) and Dhoni (38). Yuvraj and Dhoni had strike rates of 233 and 200 respectively, the major difference being that the former hit five sixes including a 119-metre-long one off the bowling of Stuart Clark and the latter, only one. Australia lost the match by 15 runs, but not before they had put a fight led by Mathhew Hayden and Andrew Symonds.

As a leader, Dhoni was widely appreciated in the media for his two fantastic moves. He gambled by asking Sreesanth to bowl his fourth and final over. The bowler uprooted Matthew Hayden's off stump after having bowled the dangerous Adam Gilchrist in the initial part of the innings. When 30 runs were needed from three overs, Dhoni introduced Harbhajan, who dismissed Clarke and conceded just three. In the penultimate over, RP Singh gave away five runs. Suddenly, the match went beyond Australia's control and it was all over very soon.

If Yuvraj had piloted India to a good score, the outcome had been masterminded by Dhoni. After the match was over, the new Indian skipper said, 'I play according to my expectation. I don't want others to fix that level of expectation. When we go back to the hotel, we should know that we gave our best. It's not for others to fix expectations—that only adds pressure. We're coming directly from England, so we don't know the expectations—in a way that has helped us.' That was the analysis of a confident man, one who knew that he wanted to win the tournament badly and also that the team, which hadn't been placed under the limelight because of their World Cup debacle, had benefitted from the absence of hype. After the semis win, one match stood between India and the trophy: the finals against Pakistan.

Both India and Pakistan had experienced astonishing exits from the 50-over World Cup only sometime ago, which made the finals between the traditional rivals an even more special occasion than usual. Before the match began, the Indian skipper had made a statement, 'The crowd will enjoy the final against Pakistan. You can expect healthy rivalry and a great game of cricket.' That turned out to be a prophecy.

The two teams met at Johannesburg. Dhoni, after winning the toss, decided to bat. Gambhir scored a fine 54-ball 75 before being dismissed in the 18th over. But India suffered major setbacks with Uthappa, Yuvraj and Dhoni getting dismissed cheaply. Sharma scored a quick 30 not out from 16 balls. At the end of 20 overs, India reached 157 for 5, the sort of score Pakistan would have settled for before the match began.

RP Singh sent back Mohammad Hafeez and Kamran Ali for 1 and a duck respectively. That started a collapse, and Pakistan stumbled their way to 77 for 6 after 11.4 overs. But Misbah was still there. Harbhajan, who had given away 18 runs in his first 2 overs, gave away 19 in his third, courtesy a Misbah special including three sixes. Pakistan needed 20 runs from 2 overs. Singh bowled the 19th over and gave away 7, scalping Umar Gul. In the key last over, Pakistan needed 13 runs with 1 wicket in hand.

Thus began the climax and Dhoni had to take an important call. Singh, Irfan and Sreesanth had finished their spells. Harbhajan's morale was low. So, Dhoni opted for the seam of Joginder Sharma. Sharma almost let him down with a wide first delivery. Dhoni, unruffled, spoke to his man for a moment. The next ball went for nothing. But the delivery that followed was a shocker, a full-toss which Misbah bludgeoned for a six. 6 runs, 4 balls: for India, a defeat seemed inevitable.

That's when Misbah made an error, which will haunt him for the rest of his life. Responding to a delivery that was full in length and on the stumps, he went for a scoop over short fine-leg. Sreesanth ran and took the catch. With his dismissal, Pakistan had lost the match by five runs. India had not only beaten them, but also won the inaugural ICC World Twenty20. Indian sports channels that had been flogging the Prudential World Cup triumph way back in 1983 finally had the footage of a second world title made possible by the efforts of a bunch of young men led by the Ranchi boy. Chappell might have not been the best coach Indian cricket could have had. But his belief that Dhoni had it in him to lead the country had turned out to be right.

After the match ended, it was time for euphoric celebrations. Indian players did the traditional lap around the ground. Signs of sportsmanship were evident when Indian and Pakistani players congratulated each other. While everybody indulged in celebrations, Dhoni was the only calm guy on the field. But he did give rise to one special moment that cricket lovers will remember for a long time. He took off his team shirt and gave it away to a fan. He moved around bare-chested, his more-Caribbean-than-Indian swagger visible to everyone present.

During the awards ceremony, the victorious skipper said, 'It's one of the things I will treasure for the rest of my life. I'd like to congratulate the boys and thank them for the response they have given me.' He explained his decision to give the crucial last over to Sharma, 'Bhajji (Harbhajan) was not 100 per cent sure of getting yorkers in the death. I thought I should throw the ball to someone who really wants to do well in international cricket. Jogi did a really good job.'

India's trophy-winning triumph at the World Twenty20 took everybody by surprise. As soon as the unexpected came true, the young Indian captain was under the limelight like never before. His decision to hand over the ball to Sharma was universally recognised as a manifestation of an inborn quality of every successful skipper: one that we refer to as the 'gut feeling'. During a felicitation ceremony in Mumbai's Wankhede Stadium later, Dhoni admitted that Misbah's moment of self-sacrifice was a cause for concern for him as well. He said, 'When Misbah-ul-Haq played that shot, my initial fear was that it might land just behind Sreesanth. So I was not looking at Sreesanth, my eyes were on his hands, whether he could catch it.' As it turned out, Sreesanth held on to it, resulting in arguably the most important triumph since the win against the West Indies way back in 1983 in the Prudential World Cup finals.

Ever since he started out as the leader of the Indian team, Dhoni's frankness has come to the fore time and again. The same quality was evident when he spoke about his 'little nervousness' as a first-time captain. But he explained, 'I think a little nervousness at this level is justified. But the way all 15 players responded, I hardly had a reason to worry.' He said, 'Whoever I tossed the ball to fetched me wickets. Whoever walked out to bat, scored the runs. So the pressure was considerably less on me. Besides, the entire team had full faith in each other's abilities and that's important.'

Dhoni's outstanding rise was a subject of discussion among Team India watchers. Praising those who came from small towns, he said, 'Guys coming from small-time towns are generally mentally and physically tougher than those coming from the metros. Smaller towns lack infrastructure and facilities. So players from there have to work harder.' However, he went on to add that the players had clicked irrespective of their backgrounds becaue of their hunger to succeed. 'Whether it's the small-town guys or those from the metros, everyone wanted to perform at the international stage and they have been successful.'

Dhoni's emergence as a leader had resulted in a memorable outcome. It convinced Harsha Bhogle that Dhoni could become a long-distance runner and the pivotal decision-maker of the Indian team. Reflecting on the early days, Bhogle remembers, 'The first time I thought he would go far was when I asked Rahul Dravid why they bat Dhoni down the order and not up at number three where he had made such a spectacular start, Rahul said that they really rated him as a finisher. To me, that was indicative of the respect earned. That is when I thought there was something more to him than seemed apparent from a distance. But it was really his approach as a captain in the Twenty20 World Cup that convinced me that he was going to be a leader.'

Conversations with those who had seen Dhoni as a promising school-going boy is a charming experience. When their Mahi became the captain, all of them were sure that he would bring the World Twenty20 trophy back home. Banerjee, his physical education teacher, says, 'The moment he got a chance to captain, I knew that he would win the cup.' Bhattacharya, his first coach, affirms, 'Even if he did not manage to pull it off in his first tournament as a skipper, I was convinced that he will win at least one World Cup for the country someday.' Sanjeev, his first captain, remembers, 'When India reached the semis, I was sure that Mahi with his team will bring this World Cup home.'

Back home, his parents ignored the local media and fans, who had gathered outside his house. They hadn't forgotten the memories of vandalism. When one speaks to remote acquaintances—ones who claim to have known him, in other words—some insist that reaching the family is very easy. One glance at their faces is enough to suggest that they aren't being entirely honest. The residence is a guarded fortress. Dhoni is known to be in love with his hometown, which is why he chose to build his permanent residence there instead of some other city.

Some might deduce that his parents have been forced to sacrifice a great deal of freedom which they once had. Indeed, they have, which is not surprising since their son's popularity in the city is such that his fans were planning to construct his temple a few years ago.

Every superstar has to pay a price for being a celebrity. Whenever Dhoni comes home, everybody who is somebody—or even nobody—wants to meet him. Politicians, the media and acquaintances among whom are those who complain that he picks and chooses among local people line up for meeting their star. Ever since he made an impact as a player, his presence in major functions lights up the occasion like nothing else can. When he made an appearance on the balcony of his residence after India's win at the 2010 ICC World Cup, there was a stampede in which several fans were injured.

But that was not the end of the Dhoni saga. Many more stories would be written very soon.

CHALLENGES AFTER TRIUMPH

DHONI'S CAREER AS a skipper had taken off with the World Twenty20 win. But his career as the captain in the one-day format didn't begin in an equally dramatic fashion. Playing against the visiting Australian team in the 2007-08 season, India lost the series 2-4. Dhoni had three decent scores of 58, 33 and 50 not out in the initial matches. But he couldn't sustain that tempo while the team found itself at the receiving end most often.

Dhoni's moves as a leader weren't subjected to criticism. India had lost to a better side. At the press conference after the final match, Dhoni admitted, 'If I look at Twenty20, we had a very young side. So keeping the intensity going throughout the 20 overs was never a problem. But over here you have to keep the guys on their toes.' Interestingly, Dravid, who had had a terrible run with the bat in the first six matches, didn't feature in the playing eleven of the last match. When asked whether keeping him out was a tough decision, Dhoni came up with a diplomatic response, 'Well he was rested.' The listener was free to draw his own conclusions. But Dhoni on his part said nothing more. India beat Australia in the one-off Twenty20 match, a reminder that they were a superior side in the shortest version of the game.

The one ugly memory of the series is the racism row that erupted after Man of the Series Andrew Symonds, who had been in spectacular form, said that he had been subjected to 'monkey' chants by the crowd during the fifth ODI in Vadodara. An Australian cameraman reported similar chants in Nagpur, the venue for the sixth ODI. In their endeavour to do some damage control, the then BCCI President, Sharad Pawar, and the chairman of Cricket Australia, Creagh O'Connor, issued a joint statement stating that racism had 'no place for it in cricket—either on or off the field.'

With Dhoni captaining the team in the shorter versions, the new dilemma for the selectors was finding the right man for the Test job, since Dravid had resigned. After Tendulkar refused to take it up, Anil Kumble was asked to captain the side for the first time ever. The decision was a popular one, the veteran spinner, who was renowned for being a thorough gentleman, having played a major part in numerous Indian wins both at home and overseas. Dhoni at twenty-six was seen as too young and inexperienced for the job. But his appointment as the vice-captain was an unofficial declaration that he had been identified as the successor to Kumble, who wasn't expected to play for a very long time.

Towards the end of 2007, Pakistan visited India. First on the menu was the five-match ODI series. India began the series with a win in Guwahati, with Dhoni being the Man of the Match because of his 77-ball 63. He came in to bat at number four instead of the usual six or seven, and explained that he was 'quite flexible' about his own position in the batting order. The decision paid off, and he got out with India merely 15 runs short of the target in a tricky chase.

After Pakistan pulled off a miraculous win in the second

tie, India hit back by winning the third one by 46 runs, the highlight being a partnership of exactly 100 runs between Yuvraj (77) and Dhoni (49). The victory notwithstanding, he spoke about the highs and lows, mentioning Yuvraj's stellar show in particular and room for overall improvement in the same breath. 'I think we bowled better than them but there is still room for improvement in this department. The fielding however, I don't think was upto the mark. Overall, you can call it an average day in the office in these departments.'

In the fourth one at Gwalior, the two of them piloted India to a win by six wickets with another century stand. Pakistan won the fifth match in Jaipur, but India won the series 3-2 against their arch-rivals. Almost as relevant as India's win was Dhoni's captaincy. With his imaginative field changes and use of bowling resources, he came across as a confident young man, who was prepared to break the stereotype. When asked about the losses and gains for India in the series, he even showed his jovial side. 'Well, I think we lost two Man of the Match awards, which they won. On what we gained, I think we won the series and the trophy.' However, he didn't make any effort to conceal his team's weaknesses as and when questions were asked. Beneath his exterior was a man with a critical mind who knew that a few problems had to be addressed and solutions found for them. These are the signs of any quality skipper.

With the ODI series out of the way, Kumble debuted as the Test skipper at the Feroz Shah Kotla in Delhi and even picked up the Man of the Match award for his seven-wicket haul in a six-wicket Indian win. Once again, Dhoni played a significant knock of 57 in the first innings after India lost its first 5 wickets for 93. Dhoni's partnership with Laxman (72 not out) steered the team out of trouble and helped it reach 276, which was the turning point in the match. The second match in Eden was a high scoring draw, remembered best for Ganguly, who made 102, his first ever international century in front of his home crowd. Dhoni, who played two useful knocks in the match, had to stay away from the final test at Bangalore. Karthik replaced him as the man behind the wickets.

For the third Test, the team travelled to Bangalore. This match belonged to Ganguly. He scored his first ever double century in a knock which evoked memories of his grand days with the bat. The match ended in a draw, but India defeated Pakistan for the first time in a home series since 1979-80. Kumble's elevation to captaincy had arrived very late in his career, but he had started out well. Now, it was time for an Australian tour, which everyone knew was going to be a tough one for the Indian team. The schedule included four Test matches, the Commonwealth Bank ODI series also featuring Sri Lanka, and a one-off Twenty20 match.

Playing for the Border–Gavaskar Trophy towards the fag end of December 2007, India was massacred by 337 runs in the first Test at Melbourne. After scoring 532 in the first innings, to lead by 69 runs—courtesy Tendulkar's unbeaten 154 and Laxman's 109—India still managed to lose the second Test at Sydney by 122 runs. This Test was marred by a pathetic umpiring error by Steve Bucknor—Symonds, who was on 30, had edged an Ishant Sharma delivery to Dhoni behind the stumps. Indians appealed for a caught behind decision, but Bucknor turned it down. Later, all hell broke loose after Symonds himself admitted that he did indeed edge the ball. The all-rounder went on to score an unbeaten 162.

Another episode that made news was that Harbhajan was

alleged to have hurled a racist slur at Symonds. Match referee Mike Procter decided to find a solution after the end of the match. The matter snowballed into a huge issue and there was a three-match ban against Harbhajan. The BCCI decided to act and it was eventually agreed that a final hearing would be conducted later. Meanwhile, Bucknor was replaced by Billy Bowden for the third Test at Perth.

Dhoni's keeping had been decent, but his form with the bat reflected in his scores: 0, 11, 2 and 35. The third Test saw a sudden reversal and India won by 72 runs. Although Dravid scored a fine 93, Irfan Pathan with his two knocks of 28 and 46 and a five-wicket match haul won the Man of the Match award. Dhoni scored 19 and 38, the latter a reasonable knock which would eventually be his highest in the series. The final Test ended in a boring draw, but Dhoni's series as a Test batsman proved to be a disaster. He somehow crawled his way to 141 runs at an average of 17.62, which was not the kind of performance he would have expected from himself. After India was dismissed for 74 in the solitary Twenty20 outing and Australia raced to a nine-wicket win, Dhoni's failure to deliver a positive result as the captain didn't help him either.

For the ODI series, Laxman and Ganguly were dropped. Dravid, who had broken a finger in Adelaide, was kept out of the squad, the result being that Tendulkar was the only senior player in the side. Soon, action in the tri-series began. The first two matches didn't deliver any result. But Dhoni, who showed some sort of form against Australia with his 37, made a convincing 88 not out against the Lankans. The Australians met India at Melbourne thereafter. The ever-so unpredictable Ishant Sharma picked up 4/38, a spell that played a huge role in limiting their total to 159. India struggled their way to 160 for 5 in 45.5 overs. Rohit Sharma paced his innings superbly to score a 61-ball 39 not out, while Dhoni scored an unbeaten 17 from 54 balls to take the team home.

India lost the next match to Sri Lanka by eight wickets, and followed that up by losing to Australia by 50 runs. India won the next crucial tie against the Lankans by two wickets, which will be best remembered by Dhoni and his fans for his innings of 50 not out that did not have a single boundary in it. Ever since his days in Ranchi and Kharagpur, where he was renowned for his ability to hit huge sixes and run quick singles and twos, Dhoni had sped like a hare between the wickets and still managed a 50 from 68 balls. After Australia beat India once again, this time by 18 runs, and also defeated Sri Lanka, the encounter between India and Sri Lanka became a must-win one for both the teams.

Dhoni made two major changes—he replaced Sreesanth with Munaf Patel and included Praveen Kumar at the expense of Virender Sehwag. Although Munaf was a failure, Praveen's inclusion was a stroke of genius. By picking up 4/31, he facilitated Sri Lanka's defeat by seven wickets and also won the Man of the Match award. After the match ended, Dhoni explained the reason behind his five-bowler strategy. 'We'd batted quite well against Sri Lanka in the past games and someone was always scoring. We just wanted to put pressure by having an extra bowler.' Now, India was in the finals, which was to be played in the best of the three formats.

The first of them at Sydney was quite simply a Sachin Tendulkar rock show. After Australia, who had been kept in check, put up 239 for 8 on the board, Tendulkar played a fascinating knock of 117 not out to anchor the team to an easy win by six wickets. In the second match at Brisbane,

India scraped through by 9 runs. Tendulkar scored 91 albeit at a slower rate as India made 258 for 9. Australia responded with 249 with Kumar justifying his skipper's trust in him by picking up another four-wicket haul to collect the Man of the Match award.

During the awards ceremony, Dhoni expressed his gratitude to Tendulkar, 'It's the toughest conditions out here. The way we improved our batting and backing each other was an important point. The way Sachin started the last few matches was at the right time. It's really good to have a team that's performing.'

Apart from saying that this was a 'greater victory than the World Twenty20,' not once did he highlight his own role. 'The role of the captain was not the only one. The captain is one guy who gathers the pressure and then channels it to the individual player and then it depends on how that individual reacts,' he said. 'We didn't start that well but we improved as the tournament went on and the credit should go to every player,' he said. He also revealed his own vision as a skipper. 'Even if we had lost this tournament, we should have stuck with the young boys. This will be the team's core.'

Instead of organizing a huge display to celebrate the win, the Board chose to have a relaxed function within the premises of the Feroz Shah Kotla Stadium. It also rewarded the team with a gift of ₹10 crore. After this taxing tour came to an end and the climax was a happy one, a few things were crystal clear. Dhoni, who had excelled as a skipper and marshalled his team without losing his cool even once, could be trusted to lead India in Test matches.

In his scheme of things, no player was indispensable except Tendulkar, whose sublime skills he had idolized since his days as a youngster. He was convinced that introducing gifted youngsters, who were hungry for opportunities, was better than retaining battle-scarred veterans, who had been there, done that, and didn't have the same motivation any longer. Besides, if their reflexes had slowed down, resulting in a decline in the quality of performances, they had to go. For this young captain, taking strong decisions in selection wasn't just the right way to proceed. Instead, that was the only way to proceed.

Sporting spirit: Mahi, the kid, enjoys 'horse riding' in 1983

Once the best, always the best: Winner of the inter-school best player trophy

Winning single-handedly: Playing with a fractured hand, he pulled off a victory for his team

32 all out: Sitting with his father Paan Singh, mother Devki Devi, brother in-law Gautam Gupta and sister Jayanti, he just can't stop smiling

Rising son: Sitting inside their old MECON Colony home, his parents watch their son with bated breath

Perfect all-rounder: He still cannot resist playing carrom, an indoor sport he is very good at

Catching practice: About to catch the cell phone of one of his fans who had requested for an autograph on it during a local tournament in Ranchi

Different ball game: He gets ready for a football match at Silli near Ranchi

Dreams come true: The Indian skipper on his Harley Davidson in his hometown

One among many: Always passionate about bikes, he flaunts one of the several he owns

He plays, he prays: At the Deori Mata temple in Ranchi

Reaching out for God: He offers his prayers to the Almighty

Couple at the temple: Along with his wife Sakshi at the Deori Mata temple

Jharkhand's most wanted: The newly married Dhonis attend a party hosted by the Chief Minister of the state

At home with games: During the 34th National Games at the Mega Sports Complex in Ranchi

Bowling on a different pitch: Trying his hand at bowling at the R K Anand Lawn Bowls Stadium in Ranchi

Security first: Escorted by the cops after his arrival at the Birsa Munda Airport in Ranchi

Look at that!: Dhoni offers a picture perfect moment during his inspection of the Mega Sports Complex in Ranchi

IPL: THE GAME CHANGER

4 OCTOBER, 2014. Chennai Super Kings (CSK)—captained by Dhoni—was taking on the Gambhir-led Kolkata Knight Riders (KKR) in the summit clash of the Champions League Twenty20. Banned for suspect action after being reported twice before the finals, star spinner Sunil Narine's absence had handicapped KKR. But KKR had performed brilliantly all through, which meant that Dhoni and his men were expected to deal with a stiff challenge at the Chinnaswamy Stadium in Bangalore. What happened thereafter turned out to be its antithesis.

Batting first, KKR led by the skipper's quickfire 80 reached 180 for 6. The Kolkata franchise could have scored more but for Dhoni's master-stroke in the 19th over. Surprising everybody, he asked the young left-arm spinner Pawan Negi to bowl the crucial over. Negi, playing only his second match of the tournament, gave away two runs and took three wickets. He eventually finished with figures of 5 for 22. CSK, in response, raced away to 185 for 2 with 9 balls and 8 wickets in hand. KKR's defeat was engineered by Suresh Raina, the young Twenty20 superstar. Raina scored an unbeaten 109 from 62 balls. Dhoni, who promoted himself in the batting order to prevent any hiccups, made 23, and eventually hit the winning runs with a towering six to take his team to the second

Champions League Twenty20 win.

Ever since Dhoni called correctly and put the opposition in to bat, CSK didn't appear to have made too many glaring errors. On a day when his team had won such a coveted trophy, most captains would have stayed away from criticism. But not Dhoni, who showed that there is no room for complacence at the top while speaking during the presentation. He agreed that the game had been a fantastic one for his side, praised the efforts of Raina and Negi, but criticised his team's fielding. 'Our fielding was not up to the mark. In finals, you have to take the game to the next level. So we didn't start well,' he said, thus sending out a message to his teammates.[27]

He didn't hesitate to praise KKR's young chinaman bowler Kuldeep Yadav, who had suffered at the hands of Raina earlier. 'Kuldeep was fantastic. He is a bowler who is not afraid to toss the ball, he has got variations. He bowled really well throughout the tournament.' Yadav had been picked for the Indian squad in the home series against the West Indies. Even while Dhoni had been marshalling his CSK troops, this observation was a reflection of his endeavour to spot new talents, who could play for the nation at the highest level. Dressed in his CSK yellows, the man who spoke during the post match presentation was the skipper of Team India.

After the celebrations had taken place, the stadium erupted in joy when CSK players did a winning lap in the ground. West Indies all-rounder Dwayne Bravo did a dance routine for the crowd, while most of the other players were ecstatic and

[27]Had to stay till the end – Raina, *ESPNcricinfo.com*, 4 October 2014. http://www.espncricinfo.com/champions-league-twenty20-2014/content/story/787339.html (accessed 21 December 2014).

not at all keen to hide their feelings. Once the serious task of winning the tournament had been accomplished, Dhoni disappeared somewhere in the background. Known to shun the limelight during such occasions, he accompanied his teammates with a hint of a smile on his face. It was a familiar sight which every cricket lover would have seen many times earlier.

The 2014 Champions League Twenty20, which the Dhoni-led CSK won, featured domestic teams from Australia, India, New Zealand, Pakistan, South Africa, Sri Lanka and the West Indies. The idea of this Twenty20 tournament had come into being in 2008 after the phenomenal success of the first edition of the Indian Premier League (IPL), which merits a separate chapter simply because of its impact on the game and Dhoni's leadership of CSK in the Twenty20 format.

On 20 February 2008, the IPL was unveiled to the cricket-loving masses the world over. Consisting of eight franchises, who had a fixed salary cap which they could use to 'buy' their players in an auction to form their respective teams for the tournament. The amount of curiosity and hype the IPL generated was nothing short of unthinkable. To start with, no cricket lover would have thought that an auction would come into being in their favourite sport someday. But on 20 February 2008, it actually did. Far from being confined to dedicated sports channels, regular updates and discussions became part of the menus of various news channels, which went on an overdrive.

Launched by the BCCI, the IPL was targeted at those cricket watchers who were getting tired of the game being played as a traditional competitive sport with no frills. Such individuals wanted to see power hitting in which the bowler was usually at the receiving end. The IPL had been designed to cater to that segment of the population. Music in the stadium added to the excitement and so did the cheerleaders. For the professional cricket player, whose flair was tailor-made for the format, the IPL arrived as a boon which made him richer by thousands of dollars or even more.

The first auction resulted in many unpredictable decisions regarding the franchises' preferences for certain players, and also the manner in which several established stars had to be satisfied with smaller sums of money. Those participating in the buying process for their respective franchises were new to the system of recruiting players. Too much money was at stake, and each one of them had devised their personal strategies to get their team formations right.

But there was one player who, everybody knew, would give rise to a battle among the franchises. It was Dhoni, who had started out with a base price of $400,000. The young Indian skipper was eventually bought by Chennai Super Kings for $1.5 million, the highest amount for any player paid by N Srinivasan's India Cements. Lalit Kumar Modi, Chairman and Commissioner, IPL, described the occasion as a historic one. Speaking to *The Hindu*, he said, 'M.S. Dhoni, Andrew Symonds and Ishant Sharma were bid by all the franchise owners. I am happy that the Indians have been picked up, and picked up well. They are all world-class players. It was a competitive round (for batsmen).'[28] While the battle over Ishant was a major surprise, the Dhoni story went along expected lines. His ability to tear the opposition's attack to shreds was

[28]'Dhoni gets the highest bid at IPL auction', *The Hindu*, 21 February 2008. http://www.thehindu.com/todays-paper/tp-sports/dhoni-gets-the-highest-price-at-ipl-auction/article1206202.ece (accessed 21 December 2014).

known to everybody. No player came anywhere close to him as a finisher. Above everything else, he had proved his leadership skills, which made him a dream buy for any team.

During the period before the IPL's first edition, the hype was such that the masses were desperately waiting for the tournament to begin. That's when Graeme Smith's men came calling. The first Test match played in Chennai was marked by high scores in which Sehwag scored a triple century. At the Motera in Ahmedabad, South Africa demolished India by an innings and 90 runs. But the third Test had an unusual twist in the Dhoni narrative. Kumble had to withdraw after suffering a groin injury, and the young wicketkeeper-batsman made his debut as the skipper of the Test team at Kanpur.

South Africa batting first scored 265, and India led by 60 runs after putting up 325 on the board. In the second innings, the South Africans were dismissed for 121. India went past the target with eight wickets in hand. Dhoni, on his part, displayed his knack for making unusual bowling decisions once again. Going for the kill in the second innings, he first asked Harbhajan to open the bowling with Ishant Sharma. The off-spinner (4/44) did a fine job. Sehwag bowled 8.5 overs to capture 3/12. Ishant (2/18) and Sreesanth (1/9) ensured that none of the batsmen could breathe easily. The series ended in a tie.

His debut as a Test skipper notwithstanding, his responses after the end of the match revealed the calm but shrewd manner in which he had gone about his task. Explaining his decision to use Sehwag on a turning track, he told the media later, 'Viru is much more than a part-timer on this kind of wicket. He continuously kept bowling the right areas, in the rough. It was a deliberate move, and we knew that with him and Yuvraj in the team we would not need an extra spinner.' Such a response seemed to indicate that, as the leader of the team in the longest version, his basics were in the right place. After the series, a new chapter in the history of international cricket was about to begin. It was time for the IPL.

The format of IPL was a simple one. Each franchise team plays the others twice, once at home and once away, followed by the semis and the final. CSK under Dhoni's leadership has a fantastic record in the tournament so far. In 2008, when the tournament began, Dhoni had to face two challenges. He had to create a cohesive unit out of CSK which included foreign players, a tough task for those who had not captained sides with members from different cricketing cultures earlier. Besides, his $ 1.5 million salary was a record which others could only hope to match someday. Dhoni, in other words, knew that he had to go out there and prove that he was worth it.

Soon, the IPL began. The first match between KKR and Royal Challengers Bangalore had one extraordinary innings: the one played by the New Zealander Brendon McCullum, who hit thirteen sixes on his way to 158 not out. RCB went down without offering any serious resistance. McCullum's innings promised many such batting rock shows in future. What more could the viewer have asked for?

The Dhoni-led CSK went through highs and lows before meeting Deccan Chargers in a match which it simply had to win to go through to the semis. If CSK lost, Mumbai Indians would have sealed a semifinal berth. The DC–CSK match went to the final over. CSK won only after Raina hit a six with four balls to spare. After this result, the semi-final line-up featured Rajasthan Royals (RR) against Delhi Daredevils (DD) while CSK had to get Kings XI Punjab (KXIP) out of the way to secure a place in the finals in Mumbai. Both the encounters turned out to be pitiably one-sided. DD were blown away by RR who won by 105 runs. In the second, KXIP tottered their way to 112 for 8 which CSK surpassed with nine wickets in hand. After watching the shocking demolition jobs in the semis, Twenty20 fans were expecting to see a great last match.

Viewed as the underdogs before the tournament began, RR, led by the legendary spinner Shane Warne, pulled off a grand result. They defeated CSK by three wickets by scoring the winning runs from the last delivery of the match. Batting first, CSK had set a reasonable target of 163 for 5. Raina led the scorer's list with a 43. Dhoni scored a quick 29 not out from 17 balls to make the target just a little bit more difficult.

The last over was a tricky one. Only eight runs were needed from it which, in an ordinary Twenty20 situation, would have been easy to chase down. RR's big problem was that they had Warne and Pakistan's Sohail Tanvir at the crease. Veteran medium pacer Laxmipathy Balaji, whose ability to alter the speed of his deliveries was well known, had been summoned to bowl. Tanvir scored the winning run in an incredibly tight finish to take the RR home.

Composed and graceful in victory and defeat, Dhoni praised Warne's leadership skills. He took the outcome in his stride sounding characteristically unperturbed. 'You win a few, lose a few. I like to remain in the middle lane and not get carried away by success or devastated by defeat. Sports is (meant) to be enjoyed,' he told Sportstar.[29] After the tournament

---

[29] *Sportstar*, 'Rajasthan Royals nails a thriller' Nandakumar Marar, 7 June 2008. http://www.sportstaronnet.com/tss3123/stories/20080607501600800. htm

got over, nobody questioned his price tag, the young skipper having led his team well and batted brilliantly to score 414 runs at an average of 41.40 with a strike rate of 133.54.

The IPL's background, impact and controversies need a separate book today. However, since it is essentially a domestic T-20 extravaganza with a twist, here is how Dhoni and his team have performed in it down the years. After going down in the finals of the first edition in 2008, 2009 took them a step backward as their most expensive player Andrew Flintoff was ruled out of the season after playing only three matches. They reached the semis before losing to RCB by six wickets. Dhoni, who had promoted himself to number three, scored a 30-ball 28, which didn't do much to help the cause of the team.

In 2010, Dhoni and his men finally won the title by beating Mumbai Indians (MI) by 22 runs in the final. Faced with the task of going past CSK's 168 for 5, MI ended up with 146 for 9. The West Indian marauder Kieron Pollard tried to make a match of it, but he was dismissed after a quickfire 27. When the South African bowling all-rounder Albie Morkel bowled at him, Dhoni made a shrewd change in the field. Pollard, who plays a high-risk game, fell for it and went back, thus ending whatever hopes MI might have had of winning the match. An ESPNcricinfo.com report noted, 'Morkel bowled a tight 19th over, with a long-off, and a mid-off up in the circle and so straight it was almost behind him. Pollard hit a catch to him: it just highlighted which captain had got it right on the night.[30]' The man leading the opposition that lost

---

[30]Raina, Dhoni star in Chennai triumph, *ESPNcricinfo.com*, Sidharth Monga, 25 April 2010. http://www.espncricinfo.com/ipl2010/content/story/457227.html (accessed 21 December 2014).

was one Sachin Tendulkar.

While getting his crucial unbeaten 57 in the finals, Raina went past Adam Gilchrist to become the highest run-getter among all the players in the IPL. Four years after he played that knock, he has become a major force in the shorter version of the game, which is the outcome of the trust his skipper has shown in him. The young southpaw has always acknowledged that Dhoni mainly advises him to keep it simple, which has enabled him to work on his strengths and develop them. His focused approach has allowed him to evolve as a batsman and actually become an important cog in the wheel of the Indian squad.

Back in 2010, however, Raina's shortcoming was the kind of problems he faced while dealing with the short-pitched delivery. For his skipper, the year proved to be a great one in the domestic Twenty20 format. Not only did CSK win the IPL, he also led the team to a Champions League Twenty20 triumph in South Africa. In the finals, the Super Kings met the Chevrolet Warriors, a South African team led by Davy Jacobs. Batting first, the home team struggled to reach 128 for 7 in their alloted quota of 20 overs. Spinners Muttiah Muralitharan (3/16) and Ravichandran Ashwin (2/16) proved to be virtually unplayable. CSK replied with a 103-run opening partnership between Michael Hussey and Murali Vijay. After Vijay was out for 58, followed by Raina, who lost his wicket after scoring just 2, Dhoni (17 not out) joined Hussey (51 not out) to end the game with one over left and eight wickets in hand.

CSK destroyed the South African champion team with such ease that a viewer should have been forgiven for thinking that the match was being played in the former's home soil. Dhoni's captaincy was immaculate, the standout moment being his introduction of off-spinner Ravichandran Ashwin in the sixth over. Ashwin dismissed Jacobs, who was looking decidedly dangerous, which not only slowed down the Warriors' scoring rate but also had a significant impact on the team's performance with the bat. After the match ended, Dhoni was asked how he managed to keep his cool. He replied, 'There is a dressing room to show your emotions. As a captain, you are as good as your side. This is a very good bunch of people and as a captain you just want to channel all the energy into the same direction. The players put in great effort and frankly it feels very good to be the captain of Chennai Super Kings.' Not surprising, since he had been able to unite the franchise players into a performing unit which sought to win without letting their emotions run riot on the field. Calling this the Dhoni effect wouldn't have been inappropriate.

In 2011, CSK put up 205 for 5 against RCB in the finals. The central character in their scorecard was opener Vijay, who made a fascinating 52-ball 95 which included six sixes and four hits to the fence. RCB, in reply, struggled to reach 147 for 8, resulting in an easy 58-run win for Dhoni's men. Although Vijay picked up the Man of the Match award, Ashwin, who bowled the first over for CSK, played a pivotal role in the win. Not only did he bowl a miserly four-over spell in which he conceded only 16 runs—which is really special in a batsman-friendly format—he dismissed the free-scoring marauder Chris Gayle for a duck. Gayle had been batting with such consistency in the series that he went on to win the Player of the Series award in spite of this flop show, and his dismissal impacted the momentum of RCB thereafter.

Known to be a bundle of endless energy, Dhoni revealed his human side when he admitted that playing in the IPL just after the World Cup wasn't easy. He also thanked the fans who had been with the team during India's historic World Cup triumph. 'The whole of India wanted the country to win the World Cup and we did. The fans were a bit emotionally drained after the World Cup to come out in large numbers initially in the IPL. But they later came out to watch the IPL,' he said.

Vijay's performance with the bat had been hardly noteworthy before the finals. In the finals, he came good and impacted the verdict with his 95 which formed the cornerstone of his 159-run opening stand with Michael Hussey. During the post match ceremony, Dhoni, who had persisted with Vijay in the opener's slot, said, 'Well you can say we saved the best for the last. Vijay and Hussey gave us a great start and stayed till the 15-16th over. Hence we could maintain the momentum and score over 200 runs,' he said.

Dhoni's move of the match was using Ashwin to bowl the opening over, a role which the latter had been asked to play earlier as well. Gayle went back in the first over itself, which proved to be the turning point. Speaking to *The Hindustan Times*, the spinner praised his skipper but for a different reason: his wicketkeeping against his bowling. By 2011, Dhoni was easily among the best keepers against spinners in the world. When called upon to remove the bails with the batsman out of crease, he was matchless. Speaking about his skipper's support as a keeper, Ashwin said, 'With Dhoni, the caught-behinds and stumpings have gone up many notches in my bowling. He understands the trajectory, the variation and the bounce that I get.'[31] At a time when the focus was usually on his leadership and batting skills, praise for his keeping from a teammate was a compliment Dhoni might have liked to hear. Unfortunately, both for CSK and him, the Champions League Twenty20 was a complete washout. CSK won just one out of four matches to languish at the bottom of their table, not the sort of verdict any leading skipper would have been satisfied with.

Pretty much the best performer at the IPL under Dhoni's captaincy, CSK entered the finals in 2012 once again. What they did not expect was that a virtually unknown player named Manvinder Bisla, playing for their opponents KKR, will shed all inhibitions and score a 45-ball 82 to help his team go past CSK's more-than-competitive score of 190 for 3. In a classic nailbiter, KKR won the match by five wickets with two deliveries left. Out of nowhere, Bisla had emerged as the star. Dhoni summarised the verdict with precision, 'Cricket is a game of plus ten minus ten. It is always like that.' He added, 'I am happy with our performance.' That happiness would abandon him after CSK fared badly at the Champions League Twenty20, although they finished with two victories and two defeats in the group stage which was better than the previous matches.

In the 2013 season, history repeated itself. CSK met MI in the finals with the latter eyeing their first title. In spite of Pollard's brutal assault during his 32-ball 60, MI could barely

[31]'I knew Gayle wouldn't step out to me at all', *The Hindustan Times*, Dinesh Chopra, 30 May 2011. http://www.hindustantimes.com/news-feed/chunk-ht-ui-cricket-interviews/i-knew-gayle-won-t-step-out-to-me-at-all/article1-703487.aspx (accessed 21 December 2014).

manage 148 for 9, which didn't seem enough. But their bowlers went on a rampage, and before one knew, CSK had been reduced to 39 for 6. Just when many had started believing that this match would produce the most one-sided final ever, in came Dhoni. He attacked with a ferocity none could have imagined. Although Dhoni remained not out with a 45-ball 63 inclusive of five sixes and three fours, the star finisher in him watched in dismay as there was a procession at the other end. CSK eventually fell short of the target by 23 runs.

CSK's bowlers had done a fine job, but their batsmen brought them to their knees. Undeterred, the skipper had waged a lonely war. A Firstpost.com report summarised, 'It was an incredible show of character from Dhoni—refusing to give up after seeing his team put in their worst performance on the biggest stage. Even in the last over, when CSK required 42 runs to win, Dhoni managed to hit Pollard for two sixes and a four. But eventually, it was for nothing.'[32] Coach Fleming said he was 'perfectly happy' with Dhoni's batting, and explained his role which underlined his importance not just for CSK but for Team India as well. 'He is there to win the game for us,' he told ESPNcricinfo.com, 'We have other players who should have put us in a position to win. They didn't do that. So he had to recover (from) the situation.'[33] The bright aspect was that CSK had reached four out of five IPL finals,

---

[32]'Mumbai beat CSK by 23 runs to win maiden IPL title', *Firstpost. com*, Pulasta Dhar, 27 May 2013. http://www.firstpost.com/sports/ ipl/mumbai-beat-csk-by-23-runs-to-win-maiden-ipl-title-817227.html (accessed 21 December 2014).
[33]'Happy with where Dhoni batted—Fleming', *ESPNcricinfo.com*, http://www.espncricinfo.com/indian-premier-league-2013/content/ story/638003.html (accessed 21 December 2014).

a tribute to the team's consistency, which was miles ahead of any of its counterparts.

What neither Dhoni nor his team members would have asked for is the spot-fixing scandal which erupted out of the blue and threatened the the very existence of the team. At the centre of it all was Gurunath Meiyappan, the son-in-law of the BCCI President N Srinivisan. Meiyappan was arrested after allegations of betting in the last week of the IPL 2013, and that, predictably, snowballed into a huge issue. Since Srinivasan is the managing director of India Cements, which owns CSK, the issue of conflict of interests concerning his ownership of the CSK and holding a position of power in the BCCI at the same time was raked up.

Although projected as the Team Principal, India Cements issued a formal press statement which stated that Meiyappan didn't hold any powerful post with the franchise. It read, 'Mr. Meiyappan is neither the owner, nor the CEO/Team Principal of the Chennai Super Kings. [He] is only one of the members (Honorary) of the management team of the Chennai Super Kings.' An article in *The Hindu* with the caustic headline 'CSK owners become Cover-up Super Kings' stated: 'With the swirling storm set off by police investigations into the spot-fixing of Indian Premier League cricket fixtures now reaching their front door, Chennai Super Kings owners N. Srinivasan and Gurunath Meiyappan moved to firewall their multi-billion rupee franchisee from potential termination by declaring that the latter had no formal association with the team.'[34]

The Champions League 2013 arrived on time. The Dhoni-

[34]'CSK owners become Cover-up Super Kings', *The Hindu*, 25 May 2013. http://www.thehindu.com/news/national/csk-owners-become-coverup-super-kings/article4746420.ece. [Access date?]

led outfit performed well but stopped one step short of the finals when Rajasthan Royals, steered by young batsman Ajinkya Rahane's 70 and spinner Praveen Tambe's brilliant spell of 3 for 10, went past them in the semis by 14 runs. Dhoni, during the post match presentation ceremony, expressed his satisfaction with the bowling, but he made no effort to disguise his disappointment with the batting performance in general. 'We did well at the start but we have to think on our batting order.' The message was loud was clear.

Dhoni had to court unnecessary limelight when many questioned his refusal to respond to questions regarding fixing and betting controversies during interactions with the media. The CSK skipper was among the witnesses who had been interviewed by the Mudgal Commission headed by former Punjab and Haryana Chief Justice Mukul Mudgal, which had been appointed to investigate the matter. The petitioner, who had challenged Srinivasan's right to hold on to his BCCI post, accused him of lying about Meiyappan later. When this issue was brought up, the BCCI counsel countered it by specifying that Dhoni's position was that Meiyappan didn't have a role in CSK's cricket-related matters.

The Mudgal Commission report stated: 'Mr. M.S. Dhoni, Mr. N. Srinivasan and officials of India Cements took the stand that Mr. Meiyappan had nothing to do with the cricketing affairs of Chennai Super Kings and was a mere cricket enthusiast supporting CSK.' This was that one sub-plot in his cricketing career that Dhoni could have done without. But then, the shadow of match-fixing had cast its spell on cricket earlier, which is why the allegations surprised few.

With IPL 2014, the cricketing action continued. Dhoni's CSK reached the semi-final stage in which Virender Sehwag, on the rampage for KXIP, scored a century and helped the latter set a target of 227 runs. Suresh Raina took everyone's breath away with a 25-ball 87 and Dhoni fought hard with his unbeaten 42 towards the end, but CSK fell short of the target by 24 runs. The skipper sounded quite annoyed with his team when he stated, 'I think definitely it was something we could have achieved, the reason being Suresh [and] the way he batted... I think in the middle overs there was some very irresponsible cricket by some of the most experienced international cricketers, so I think definitely we need to have a look, in a game like this when the stakes are high, you can't really commit mistakes.' CSK would regain its prestige by winning the Champions League Twenty20 a few months later.

Under his able leadership and because of his inspiring ability to win matches with the bat against adversity, CSK has risen to become the best performer among the franchise teams so far. In 2008, when the IPL's story had just begun, nobody had seen this coming.

GROWING UP AS A SKIPPER

THE INDIAN PREMIER League had made an emphatic beginning in 2008. But life for a professional cricketer had to go on. Physically drained after a taxing schedule, Dhoni's men flew down to Dhaka to play Kitply Cup, a tri-nation tournament featuring Pakistan, India and the hosts Bangladesh. Hence, it was widely—and rightly—expected that India would meet Pakistan in the finals. That happened, although the decider between the two teams swung the other way after India had defeated Pakistan by 140 runs in the preliminary stage.

Pakistan, helped by tons from Salman Butt and Younis Khan, made 315 for 3. The Indian response would have made any fan absolutely livid. Out of the top eight batsmen, everyone except Sehwag reached double figures. Four among them got out in their 20s. Only Yuvraj and Dhoni scored half-centuries.

Towards the end, Dhoni, who top-scored with 64, started getting restless and disturbed. His batting partners were coming out and returning to the pavillion in a steady procession. The team needed 32 runs from 2 overs for a win. When Shahid Afridi came to bowl the forty-ninth over, Dhoni spanked the first delivery for a six. In an effort to hit an identical stroke, he fell and India lost by 25 runs. After the match, Dhoni reflected on the reason behind India's failure,

'At times you have to take a risk but [today], more often than not, the shots went straight to the fielder, who didn't have to move. The selection of shots wasn't really appropriate but at the same time you have to play shots while chasing over six an over. So we kept losing wickets even though we were scoring and we never had the momentum with us.' Not many cricket fans would have been hurt because of the team's failure though. After all, not many were following this tournament anyway.

If India were to beat Australia or South Africa by 256 runs, the outcome would have been remembered for years. India did win by such a massive margin, but against Hong Kong in the Asia Cup that followed. In the next match that was played the very next day, Pakistan gave India a scare by posting 299 for 4. But Sehwag flew to 119 from 95 balls, which allowed India to win the match with almost eight overs to spare.

Bangladesh faced a similar problem. Playing on a flat track, they managed to score 283 for 6. India coolly went past the target with seven wickets in hand and more than six overs to spare, with Raina making a century and Gambhir scoring 90. What was distinctly noticeable was India's poor show on the field. Dhoni, the leader, defended his men after the match, 'I am not really happy with the schedule. Two teams are playing back-to-back games, and two teams are not. Under these conditions, it is really tough.' He admitted, 'You could make out from the start the intensity was not there.' In his typically calm manner, he had conveyed his message of dissatisfaction. The captain's matter-of-factness would have been reassuring for the team.

What India had done in the three previous matches, Pakistan did to India in the next match. Helped by a string

of useful scores, India posed a seriously challenging total of
of 308 for 7. It was interesting to note that while Dhoni
top-scored with 76, his strike rate of 79.16 was the lowest
among the all the Indian batsmen who reached double figures.
Pakistan cruised to a shockingly easy win by eight wickets
in 45.3 overs. The batsmen milked a fatigued Indian bowling
which seemed to have lost control over what it could offer
to challenge and dismiss the batsmen, who were climbing a
mountain of runs with the ease of someone climbing a hillock
in the neighbourhood.

The pitch in Karachi was a bowler's graveyard. The average
cricket lover ought to have been forgiven for his inability
to remember the number of times 300-plus runs had been
scored. In the Sri Lanka–India tie, the latter had to win to
qualify for the finals while the former already had. In spite
of that cushion of security, the Lankans didn't relax for a split
second and scored 308 for 8. India, in reply, massacred their
bowling to score 310 for the loss of four wickets. That the
victory had been achieved with 19 balls yet to be bowled is
proof enough how easy scoring those runs must have been.
Pakistan's final match against Bangladesh at the Super Four
stage lost its meaning.

Alas, the Lankans demolished India by 100 runs in the
finals. Sri Lankans were all out for 273, and Indians, in reply,
were skittled out for 173. Sehwag adhered to his no-mercy
formula to make a 36-ball 60. Dhoni fought hard to score
49 from 74 balls. The man who caught all the damage was
the mystery spinner Ajantha Mendis, who picked up 6 for
13. Introduced to international cricket barely few months ago,
Mendis owned a peculiar mix of deliveries which included a

puzzle called 'carrom ball.'[35] Having already qualified for the final, Lankans had smartly decided not to field this youngster against India at the Super Four stage. Mendis foxed and defeated the Indians single-handedly, thus making a powerful statement of his emergence in international cricket.

Dhoni had been inviting outrageous comparisons from the beginning of his career. When he had just started winning matches, some had started suggesting—without making it official, of course—that he would surpass Ganguly's records as a skipper. His credentials as a wicketkeeper-batsman were being analysed in the context of the legendary Adam Gilchrist, and that was unfair. A former cricketer admits that while it is difficult to believe that such comparisons did not reach Dhoni's ears, how he managed to deal with them is possibly the biggest triumph of his life.

By the time Asia Cup had ended, the Indian captain, who kept wickets and batted in a significant position, was positively tired. So he requested the BCCI to rest him for the Test series against Sri Lanka. The Board agreed without raising any unnecessary question and selected Dinesh Karthik and Parthiv Patel for the tour. There were debates on whether or not a cricketer could skip national duty without any valid reason such as picking up an injury. Naturally, those who questioned the decision didn't admit to it that he could have easily faked an injury which he did not. Appreciation of honesty was simply not on their agenda.

One significant decision in the advertising world showed that Dhoni as the leader of his young men was making the ad

---

[35]It is a peculiar type of spin bowling where the ball is released by flicking it between the thumb and the middle-finger to make it turn.

gurus think about the future. Pepsi, the American soft-drink giant, chose to drop Tendulkar, who had been with them for many years, and opted for Dhoni along with the two Sharmas, Ishant and Rohit, for their 'Youngistan' campaign. Dravid and Ganguly had been dropped earlier. Times were changing, and it was high time everybody embraced the change: the message was loud and clear.

Meanwhile, Karthik and Patel failed to capitalise on the opportunity with their pathetic performances in Sri Lanka. India went down 2-1 with Mendis messing with the batsmen to pick up twenty-six wickets in the series. Now was the time for the ODI series. Kumble made way for Dhoni. And what a turnaround it was. For the first time ever, India won a bilateral series in Sri Lanka.

The 3-2 verdict in favour of India revealed a peculiar pattern. Whenever Dhoni played well, India won. When he did not, the team lost. In the first tie, which the Lankans won by eight wickets, Dhoni laboured hard to score 6 runs from 28 balls. India won the second match, a low-scoring affair, by three wickets. He scored 39. The third one which resulted in a 33-run win for India saw him score 76 runs, while the fourth, which India won by 46 runs, had a Dhoni special of 71. Sri Lanka won the final match by 112 runs after the Indian target had to be revised according to the Duckworth–Lewis method. In this match, he was dismissed for one. This connection between Dhoni's performance and the outcome was a strange one, and it certainly didn't reflect the reality in a larger context. But it did show the sheer worth of his presence in the Indian team.

Dhoni scored 193 runs at an average of 38.60, which was excellent under the circumstances. He looked fresh and lively, was dynamic on the field in his own understated way, and made a huge impact on the overall performance of the team. His contribution—both with the bat and also as a decisive skipper—was acknowledged when he received the Man of the Series award.

Expectedly, the Indian skipper was a happy and relieved man. Known to underplay his own performance as a player— there have been times when the commentators and the media have had to persuade him to talk about himself—he chose to emphasise on his team as he always does. In the process, he also defines the driving force behind his leadership. Speaking to ESPNcricinfo.com, Dhoni once said, 'A captain shares responsibilities, finds problem areas, and sends the best guy to rectify that problem. A good team makes a good captain, not the other way around. You have to let players go in the right direction; after that it is up to the individual.'[36]

Ever since he had taken over as the skipper of the ODI and Twenty20 squads, he had shown a distinct preference for youth, who he believed had the potential to deliver at the highest level. Dhoni agreed and attributed his approach to the demands of the modern-day game. 'You want to have batsmen who run quickly, who can convert ones into twos and put pressure on the fielders... If you've scored a par score and have a fielding side which is safe then you add 15-20 more runs.'

He also spoke about giving opportunities to players who had performed well at the domestic level and also during A-level tours. Such players needed to be given 'enough chances'

---

[36]'Triumphant Dhoni stresses on team effort', *ESPNcricinfo.com*, Jamie Alter, 29 August 2008. http://www.espncricinfo.com/slvind/content/story/366886.html (accessed 21 December 2014).

so that if they failed to rectify their problem areas repeatedly, they could go back and correct their shortcomings. Dhoni's emphasis on such players had a clear connect with his own background. Not only had he played for a state which didn't have a reputation for producing quality players, he had also undertaken a long journey through the route of the domestic circuit before making it to to the Indian team. Like every other player, he understood the challenges every aspiring cricketer has to face. The fact that he had to turn out for a domestic squad with virtually no record of cricketing excellence to prove his talent meant that he understood that just a little bit better than most others did.

India's win in a bilateral series against the Lankans in their home soil was their first one after twenty-three years. While Dhoni's career graph continued to evolve, his characteristics both as a skipper and a player emerged in full public view. While selecting his team, he didn't hesitate from taking tough decisions, which worked most often. As a batsman, his was an act that everybody looked up to. The leader in him had acquired a reputation for being a composed player whose attitude rubbed off on his fellow players in the field. In wins, he deflected attention from himself and focused on his colleagues. After losses, he was graceful while acknowledging his rival's superiority on any given day. When a legend like Lara had lost his cool during the bizzare episode of his controversial dismissal, he had set an example by retaining his cool and cluding questions about it later. In many ways, his conduct resurrected memories of old times when cricket was a 'gentleman's game.'

Facing the Australians at home was the next challenge on the agenda of the Indian team. After a drawn first Test at Bangalore, during which Kumble picked up an injury, Dhoni was made the stand-in skipper during the second Test at Mohali for the second time in his career. The Aussies were led by Ricky Ponting. And India, under Dhoni, did the unthinkable by thrashing the Aussies by 320 runs, the biggest margin of win by runs in their history of Test cricket.

As a skipper, Dhoni once again showed that experimentation was his middle name. Although Ganguly played the anchor's role and got a century, Dhoni came out to bat at number eight and tore into the bowling to score 92. In the second, with brisk runs required, he walked out to bat at number three and hit a quick 68 not out. He didn't hesitate to demote Dravid and sent in Ganguly at four and Tendulkar at five in the second innings. When he was on the field behind the wickets, he led a side that seemed energised and keen to put it past the Australians. His leadership came in for a lot of praise with the former Australian captain Ian Chappell suggesting that Dhoni should be leading the side for the rest of the series whether or not Kumble managed to recover from his injury.

The Indian selectors didn't take such drastic measures. But something else happened. Kumble, who returned to lead the side in the third Test at Delhi, picked up an injury on the final day. He announced his retirement, which was the most important happening in the match. For Indian cricket, this was an emotionally charged moment; Kumble, a loyal servant of the game, had won many battles for the team, never courted a controversy or sought the limelight. Now, he was going away. Taking his place was Dhoni, who had already gained enough experience in captaincy by leading the team in the two shorter versions. A day after his retirement, Kumble expressed his confidence in his successor. 'We have an able leader in Dhoni and he is perfectly suited to take over Test captaincy.

Team is also looking very nice. I am sure it will continue to move forward. Indian cricket is in safe hands,' the veteran leg-spinner told NDTV.[37] Kumble wasn't wrong.

Ranchi is the birthplace of Dhoni: and numerous Dhoni stories as well. A cab driver in Ranchi claims that his 'taxi got blocked' because a couple of hundred people had formed a group and started dancing on the streets during office hours. They held huge banners on which a line written in Hindi proudly declared, 'Humara Mahi, duniya ka pehla captain teenon khel main' (Our Mahi, the first captain in the world to lead the side in all the three formats). Banerjee, the man who discovered him, says, 'When Dhoni was made the permanent Test captain, I experienced the sort of joy which words cannot describe.'

India, under Dhoni, thrashed Australia by 172 runs in Nagpur. The Nagpur Test was the last for Ganguly, who had announced his retirement before the beginning of the series. He left the venue on the shoulders of Laxman and Harbhajan. But before that happened, Dhoni presented Ganguly with a beautiful moment on the field: a quiet emotional gesture in which he requested the great former skipper to lead the team for a few overs. 'I didn't expect MS to ask me to captain the side for five overs. I was already switched off, so he woke me up. I didn't know what was happening the first six-seven balls. Luckily, they were nine down so I managed to do it for three and then said it's his job, not mine any more,' he said later.

A great skipper, who had led India to many famous

---

[37]'Dhoni perfect for Test captaincy: Kumble', NDTV, 29 November 2008. http://sports.ndtv.com/cricket/news/71031-dhoni-perfect-for-test-captaincy-kumble (accessed 21 December 2014).

victories, Ganguly, it appeared, knew that Dhoni was his true successor. In certain ways, he saw a bit of himself in the young man. 'Captaincy is a spark, it's not just preparation or the homework, it's about the spark on the field, which MS (Dhoni) has. He's got that extra bit of luck which you require in captaincy. I have never believed too much in the drawing board. I see a lot of that in MS Dhoni. He doesn't believe much in team meetings and all. He just does what he sees on the field. He will be tested when India goes overseas and I'm sure he will live up to it.'

Whether or not Dhoni would deliver overseas was a question that only time would answer. Before that, the Nagpur Test had two moments that had nothing to do with the sport. Apart from inviting Ganguly to lead the team for a few overs, Dhoni offered his respect to Kumble, who had come down to watch the match, by inviting him to jointly receive the Border–Gavaskar trophy. Several years after the series ended, cricket lovers still remember these acts as an exemplary way of saying goodbye.

Soon after this series ended, England, led by Kevin Pietersen, came calling for a tour consisting of seven ODIs and two Tests at the fag end of December. In the ODI series, the visitors suffered five consecutive losses. That is when the bad news started coming in. Mumbai was under siege. As many as twelve coordinated attacks were taking place in the city, which had come to a standstill. The world watched with horror as terrorists spread panic and killed helpless people in an operation that was being executed after meticulous planning. Cricket was reduced to irrelevance as the English team took the next available flight and left India. The next two ODIs were cancelled. However, the Government of India as well as the BCCI was keen to make sure that the show must go on.

After a lot of request, the English team returned to India. Their decision touched the hearts of millions, who saw it as a symbol of their faith in the nation's internal security system. The venue of the first Test was shifted from Mumbai to Chennai where India chased down a challenging fourth innings target of 387 with Tendulkar hitting the winning runs to remain unbeaten at 103. Tendulkar is a Mumbai boy who had been emotionally bruised after the attacks on his city just a few days ago. That moment gave every Mumbaikar a reason to indulge in a fleeting smile. The emotional value of that boundary that took the Indian team past the target buried all the technical questions regarding the strengths and weaknesses in bowling and batting and also about Dhoni's captaincy which had been practically infallible all through.

The second Test at Mohali, which was affected by fog, ended in a tame draw. Dhoni came in for some criticism for late declaration, which gave India a maximum of 43 overs to make an attempt to dismiss England in their second innings. This issue turned into a minor highlight because India had taken the last six English wickets for 22 runs in the first innings. But the new skipper didn't hide behind any excuse to defend his decision. Speaking to ESPNcricinfo.com, he said, 'It's not always so easy. There was not much wear and tear (in the pitch). We were leading the series 1-0 and it wasn't 100 per cent sure that if we put them in to chase, we'd get them out to win the series 2-0. At the same time, we saw the importance of Gauti's (Gautam Gambhir) and Yuvraj's batting on in the match. We wanted them to score their centuries.'

Everybody was impressed with his analytical mindset when he explained, 'One more reason was when we started batting yesterday evening, we were not sure about the fog. If we'd have gone after the bowlers right from the start and lost wickets thinking that it would be a 70-over game on the last day... Suppose we turned up and found that it was okay to play at 9 am, like on the second day, and found that you had 98 overs. You would have been thinking that 350 would be a good score to set, and then you find that 98 overs are possible and 350 is easily achievable.'[38] There was a thought behind the decision. Few had seen it coming.

The start of Dhoni's career as a Test captain had been nothing short of outstanding. Out of the first five matches, he had won four and drawn the fifth, the sort of percentage even all-time greats such as Clive Lloyd and Steve Waugh would have bargained for any day. He had goals in mind, which went way beyond the team reaching the number three spot in ICC Test rankings. He was spending time with Gary Kirsten, the former South African batsman, who had been appointed the coach of the Indian team sometime ago.

Even before he had taken over from Kumble, Kirsten had expressed his confidence in the young man. According to a PTI report in NDTV, the coach had said, 'MS is a great thinker. He has got fantastic skills in terms of understanding the situation.'[39] That thinker who Kirsten truly admired was firmly at the forefront. From his childhood, he hated the thought of defeat, although his face didn't reflect how he felt

---

[38]'We wanted them to score their centuries: Dhoni', *ESPNcricinfo.com*, S Aga, 23 December 2008. http://www.espncricinfo.com/indveng/content/story/384073.html (accessed 21 December 2014).

[39]'Dhoni is ready for Test captaincy: Kirsten', NDTV, 9 September 2008. http://sports.ndtv.com/cricket/news/63939-dhoni-is-ready-for-test-captaincy-kirsten (accessed 21 December 2014).

within. His start had been electrifying and he was evidently eyeing a lot more.

The year 2009 began with a tour of Sri Lanka. In the five ODIs, India won by a convincing margin of 4-1. That Dhoni enjoyed his trip and the opposition's bowling in particular reflected in his performance with the bat. He scored 264 runs with a highest of 94 at an average of 88.66 which included three fifties and topped the batting averages.

At the end of the last match, Sri Lankan skipper Jayawardene said, 'The wicket played a major role and it allowed us to push this score. Credit to India, they played really well. We were up against a really good side.' Dhoni was as candid as ever. 'They played brilliantly. Our bowling wasn't so strong but it was good to give the guys chances. If the dressing room atmosphere is good then it brings out more talent. Really happy to play here. We won the series but it's never easy playing in SL.' That India also won the one-off Twenty20 match against the home side didn't do their morale any harm.

The tour against New Zealand that followed didn't seem to be challenging on paper. While India was ranked third, New Zealand was eighth according to the ICC Test rankings. Theoretically, therefore, there was no reason to be apprehensive but for the fact that New Zealand's was one such bastion that India had failed to conquer since 1968 when Mansur Ali Khan Pataudi had led the team to a Test series triumph. Arguably the best strategist that Indian cricket has ever seen, Pataudi told the media in Bhopal: 'The team led by captain Mahendra Singh Dhoni is the best team in the history of Indian cricket and is capable of winning the Test series in New Zealand.' The statement had an element of surprise and yet, nobody would have taken it lightly.

The tour started badly, with India losing both the Twenty20 matches. Things started to look better after the five-match ODI series which India won 3-1 with one match declared a 'no result' due to intervention of rain. Dhoni's men carried the momentum forward and won the first Test at Hamilton. Piloted by Tendulkar's majestic 160 in the first innings, India cruised to a ten-wicket win. Interestingly, Dhoni stuck to his formula of getting an unexpected bowler to deliver the goods for him. Yuvraj Singh, with his gentle off-spin, got rid of Brendon McCullum, who had scored 84 and looked all set to get a few more.

In the absence of Dhoni, Sehwag led the team in the second Test. India managed to earn a draw after being compelled to follow-on. The third Test at Wellington was slightly peculiar. Dhoni was back in the side. India batting first, scored 379, and New Zealand responded with 197. In spite of having a big first innings lead, India batted for a long time, leaving New Zealand with a target of 617. New Zealand escaped with a draw after the rains played spoilsport on the fifth day. Under fire for being too defensive, a criticism that would haunt him from time to time later, Dhoni explained that the team knew that it might have rained. 'But it was not certain,' he said, adding that the team didn't get even 110 overs to bowl the New Zealanders out. That argument found few buyers.

Among those who questioned Dhoni's delaying tactics was the former Indian off-spinner Erapalli Prasanna, who found it 'baffling.' Talking to *The Indian Express*, Prasanna made a significant observation about his captaincy nonetheless. 'I see a lot of Tiger (Pataudi) in Dhoni. Like Tiger, Dhoni too is not very demonstrative on the field. Tiger's every move was well planned, so is the case with Dhoni. Tiger was always ahead of the game and I see that in Dhoni as well. Most importantly, both have had the whole-hearted support of their teammates. You got to allow every player his legitimate space in the team, it's the only way to get the best out of every individual.'[40] Coming from Prasanna, who had observed Pataudi at work, this assessment was a compliment a young Dhoni would have been proud of.

After the IPL got over, the Indian team had to focus on a new destination: England. The occasion was World Twenty20. India had won the inaugural edition under Dhoni's captaincy, which made them one of the firm favourites in the second edition.

When India had won the first edition, the skipper had said that the absence of hype, which was a response to the setback in the 50-over World Cup, had allowed his team to play freely. But, circumstances had changed. So, the big question began to emerge.

What now?

---

[40]'I see a lot of Tiger in Dhoni, says Prasanna', *The Indian Express*, Shamik Chakrabarty, 10 April 2009. http://archive.indianexpress.com/news/i-see-a-lot-of-tiger-in-dhoni-says-prasanna/445352/ (accessed 21 December 2014).

MAN FOR ALL SEASONS

THE IPL WAS being increasingly seen as an area of serious concern for the Indian team. Top players would play with minor physical issues for their respective franchises, but one player, whose name hijacked the focus, was Virender Sehwag. Sehwag had been declared fit by the team physio, but it was only after he reached England that he realized he wasn't fit enough. Rumours of a rift between the skipper and the vice-captain started circulating in the media, not the kind of beginning to a tournament any Dhoni's men would have asked for.

Against this background, India's journey in the World Twenty20 began. After beating Bangladesh and Ireland easily, India faced the West Indies, who attacked the batsmen into submission with short-pitched deliveries and won by seven wickets in the third tie. Despite a bold counter-attack by Dhoni and Ravindra Jadeja towards the end, the hosts managed to win by 3 runs. In the last match in the group stages, South Africa set a measly target of 131 for India. Yet, the team was destroyed by their bowling attack and finished at 118 for 8. By the time India's campaign ended, they were a humiliated lot.

No cricketer, no matter how great, is immune to criticism. Dhoni had experienced a dose of it during India's tie against England because of his decision to send Jadeja to bat ahead of Yuvraj. During the presentation ceremony, after the loss against South Africa, he was booed by followers of Indian cricket who were present there. To his credit, he handled it remarkably well. 'It's not the first time I have been booed. When we lost in 2007 World Cup (against New Zealand), mera antim sanskar (my last rites) was also done. But I don't feel bad. It shows the expectation levels of fans,' he said. Then, he narrated an interesting anecdote, 'I was told by a senior a few years ago. He said if somebody is appreciating you, don't hit seventh heaven. If you fall on the floor, it wouldn't be good for you. So adopt a central path. I try to do so.' As years went by and he accepted cheers and jeers with the same degree of calmness, why he took this suggestion seriously became inceasingly evident.

In Ranchi, security around the skipper had to be increased after people who called themselves his fans went berserk. Immediately after India's loss against England, scores of them burnt his effigy, yelled anti-Dhoni slogans and accused him of 'under-estimating' England. *The Dawn* in Pakistan quoted a young protestor named Arun Kumar who wrote him off with a statement to the Reuters in Ranchi, 'Dhoni took the match lightly, he adopted a casual attitude... He is fascinated by the glamour world more than cricket.'[41] In his hometown, he was expected to be infallible. Any slip downwards, and he turned into a subject of condemnation and ridicule.

The taxing schedules imposed on cricketers has been a matter of discussion for years. The IPL has come into the

---

[41]'Indian media, fans furious at team's ouster', *The Dawn*, 15 June 2009. http://www.dawn.com/news/471418/indian-media-fans-furious-at-teamaes-ouster (accessed 21 December 2014).

picture, which has made the players richer but also expects them to play a lot more. In 2009, India had very little time to contemplate on the debacle as the team left for the West Indies for a four-match ODI series. The 2-1 verdict in India's favour in a series that had one no-result wasn't seen as a compensation for the disastrous show in the World Twenty20. But Dhoni batted well in all the three innings, scoring 41, 95 and 46 not out which won him the Man of the Series award. This was the fifth consecutive ODI series win for India, and the skipper avoided any mention of his own form. 'It's a pleasure to win series out of the country. The bowlers took the initiative, we have a very good bowling attack and the youngsters who came in and got a chance have proved himself,' he said.

What happened thereafter is unheard of. Playing in the Compaq tri-series against Sri Lanka and New Zealand after getting two complete months of relaxation, India became the number-one-ranked team in the world after beating New Zealand by six wickets. Twenty-four hours later, the smile disappeared from everybody's faces as Sri Lanka mauled India by 139 runs. The number one spot had to be vacated.

In the finals, Tendulkar sparkled with the bat to score a century while Dhoni and Yuvraj coming in at numbers three and four got to their half-centuries to help India set a huge target of 319 for 5. In an attacking spell, Harbhajan picked up a five-for as the Lankans went down by 46 runs. In addition to Tendulkar's 44th hundred, the win was also special for India as it had managed to win in an ODI final for only the fourth time in twenty-one attempts since 2000. Happy but determined to keep the tempo going, Dhoni said, 'Being the second-placed team in world rankings, we have to keep performing well to sustain the quality.' For the Indian skipper, complacence was not an option.

In 2009, India was on a high. Such was the team's consistency that any cricket watcher would have believed that the team had a serious chance at the ICC Champions Trophy in South Africa. But one loss against Pakistan sent them crashing out of the tournament. Depleted by the absence of Sehwag, Zaheer and Yuvraj due to injuries, India lost the tie by 54 runs. The second match against Australia which was declared a no-result due to rains proved to be decisive.

India's third tie against the West Indies was a tricky affair for the former. Even if Dhoni's men won while Australia beat Pakistan in a match being played at the same time, India would have been out of the tournament. India played brilliantly, first by limiting the West Indies to a very low score of 129 and then surpassing it by scoring 130 for 3 with 107 deliveries yet to be bowled. But Australia overcame Pakistan and India was out, having failed to reach the semis of an ICC world event for the second time in 2009. Reflecting on the outcome, Dhoni said, 'We were off the boil against Pakistan and we lost. Then we had a washout and we won the match against West Indies. I can't say if our performance was bad.' For sometime, India's batting performances had been able to cover up for its mediocre bowling and fielding lapses. Dhoni referred to these problems, but he admitted that the 'change won't happen overnight.'

Matches flew. India won quite a few, lost the others, but Dhoni's approach on the field remained as calm and understated as ever. During crises as well as wins, he seemed to be in complete control over his mind. He was getting accustomed to criticisms as well as praises. The average viewer saw him as a rock star in spite of a few shortcomings, which showed up from time to time. In press conferences, he responded to questions without getting flustered. He was a good leader to play under, his fans believed as his career progressed.

For two consecutive years, Dhoni was named the 'ICC Player of the Year' which would have given him some psychological comfort when India faced Australia in a seven-match ODI series at home in October 2009. Sehwag had returned to the team, although his 138 runs in six innings with a top score of 40 was a mediocre performance. Dhoni and Tendulkar were in excellent form. But, while India didn't make things easy for their opposition, they went down by 4-2.

The first tie at Vadodara was a cliffhanger. After having set a target of 293 for India, Australia pocketed the match with a victory margin of 4 runs. The architect of India's 354 for 7 at Nagpur was Dhoni, whose 107-ball 124 was the kind of spectacular display every cricket lover had been missing for quite sometime. So what if the innings began with the ball striking his helmet? The *Sydney Morning Herald* got it dead right when they said, 'Dhoni was very fortunate to escape with his skull intact after his first ball, when he turned his head away from a (Ben) Hilfenhaus bouncer. The ball struck the very bottom of Dhoni's helmet at the back of his head, which kept him unhurt—and definitely unshaken.'[42] He tore into the Australian attack, reminding the viewers of the young man of yesteryears who used to go on a rampage with not

---

[42]'Captain Dhoni thumps 124 as rampaging Indians pile on run record', *Sydney Morning Herald*, 29 October 2009. http://www.smh.com.au/news/sport/cricket/captain-dhoni-thumps-124-as-rampaging-indians-pile-on-run-record/2009/10/28/1256405430092.html (accessed 21 December 2014).

many exceptions. In recent times, his scoring rate, while still quick, had slowed down in comparison. That day in Nagpur resurrected old memories. Those who admired him for his hitting alone would have said that the cricketer hadn't lost his touch.

If Yuvraj's knock of 78 was the turning point of the third match in Delhi, it was Dhoni with his 71 not out who steered India to a six-wicket win. Mohali was the venue for the fourth match where Australia, after setting a not-too-difficult target of 251, went past India by 24 runs. The fifth match in Hyderabad, where India lost, will however be best remembered for a masterclass from Tendulkar.

Australia set India a huge target of 351 runs, and India came threateningly close before being all out for 347. Tendulkar's 141-ball knock of 175 should have won the match, but that didn't happen because nobody except Raina (59) played a significant supporting act. In Guwahati, Australia won by six wickets, thus winning the series 4-2 since the final tie in Mumbai was abandoned without a ball being bowled.

Dhoni failed to excel in the second half of the series. Still, he topped the batting averages and scored the maximum number of runs (285) in the series. 'We haven't backed the opportunities that we have got. A majority of the batsmen haven't contributed at the same time,' he said. 'In the games where our top order didn't perform, our middle order also didn't bat well. In the end we have lost the series. We have done well in patches in this series but we haven't grabbed the opportunities.' If unreliable bowling and fielding had let him down not long ago, this time it was the turn of the batsmen. In professional cricket, there are no stoppages. He had to accept the verdict and move on.

Towards the end of 2009, a big question was doing the rounds in the cricketing circles. Will India take the number one spot in the ICC Test rankings? It seemed possible, since Sri Lanka were going to play them at home. The first Test in Ahmedabad, a ridiculously extravagant run feast, ended in a draw. With Gambhir, Sehwag and Dravid scoring centuries at the top of the order in Kanpur, India raced to a win by an innings and 144 runs.

The third Test in Mumbai was an encore with the home team downing the visitors by an innings and 24 runs. The star of the show was Sehwag who brutalised the Lankan attack with his knock of 293. Dhoni's unbeaten 100 was a memory that deserved to be treasured, coming as it did at the Brabourne Stadium in Mumbai which hosted a Test after 36 years. *The Telegraph* described it as one of the most 'methodical innings by a wicketkeeper-batsman down the order,' which could be seen from the manner in which he had structured his innings.[43]

The first half century had a six and a four in it, but the next, as many as five sixes and two fours, were those which helped India reach their highest ever Test score of 726 for 9 (declared). Sri Lanka went past 300 twice, but that was not good enough in the end.

The Twenty20 series that followed was tied at 1-1 while its ODI counterpart resulted in an easy 3-1 win for the hosts. But the one big fact that eclipsed everything else was that India, after its second consecutive Test win at the Brabourne Stadium,

[43]'Dhoni century gives India 333-run lead—India post their highest-ever total in Tests', *The Telegraph*, 5 December 2009. http://www.telegraphindia.com/1091205/jsp/sports/story_11824088.jsp (accessed 21 December 2014).

had climbed the Everest of Test rankings. On 6 December 2009, they had been led by one MS Dhoni to the number one spot in the ICC rankings.

For the captain, this win was accompanied by a special celebration. The only worry was that India might not be able to hold on to that spot because of gaps between Test matches in the team schedule. Dhoni was in a different mood though. 'We hardly get time for ourselves... We would rather celebrate the moment than think about what we should be doing next,' he said.

As India rejoiced, the BCCI, sensing a renewal of audience interest in Tests, made adjustments to change the five-ODI series against South Africa in February into one with two Tests and three ODIs. Before that, however, there was a tri-series against Sri Lanka and Bangladesh, in Bangladesh. India beat the hosts twice and shared a 1-1 result before the finals against Sri Lanka which Dhoni's men lost.

The focus shifted to Tests, with Dhoni skipping the first one due to back pain in which Sehwag led India to victory by 113 runs. He was back in the second and final Test in Dhaka which resulted in a win by 10 wickets. Not many cricket lovers were serious about this series, but a tough battle was on the cards. South Africa was coming home.

In the first Test in Nagpur, India was blown away by an innings and 6 runs by the formidable outfit ranked second in the world. India missed the services of Dravid, Laxman and Yuvraj, who were out due to injuries. But Dhoni didn't hesitate to admit that the outstanding South African fast bowler Dale Steyn had bowled unplayable balls to the Indian batsmen who had found him very difficult to handle.

Now, it was over to Kolkata where India won, and that

too by a margin of an innings and 57 runs. The Indian innings of 643 for 6 declared had four centurions: Sehwag (165), Tendulkar (106), Laxman (143 not out) and Dhoni (132 not out). Although Hashim Amla scored centuries in both innings, the visitors were thrashed. With this win, India, which would have lost its number one ranking had it failed to win, held on to what it had achieved after such a long struggle.

After this match, ESPN Cricinfo made an interesting observation. While referring to Dhoni's unorthodox methods, such as the absence of a silly point which allowed Amla to rotate the strike without problems, the report referred to his well-maintained 'mask of composure'.[44]

Throughout his career, Dhoni has always come across as a cricketer who remains cool as ice in the toughest of situations. Is his calmness real or simply an approach which he has consciously adopted to make sure that the players could give their best irrespective of the situation the team was in? Even if Dhoni wears a mask while leading his team, he certainly wouldn't admit he does. The reality notwithstanding, there is very little doubt that this approach has generally worked for him.

India's victory in Kolkata had an interesting sidelight. Under fire for having lost his sting, Harbhajan, who had bowled really well in the match, made a statement to the media. Not known as someone who keeps his emotions in check, he attacked the media for being severe on him and his skipper. 'I have been hearing a lot of things from them (the media), but today they were on the receiving end,' he erupted without a

[44]'Grand theatre lights up Indian victory', *ESPN Cricinfo*, S Aga, 18 February 2010. http://www.espncricinfo.com/indvrsa2010/content/story/448926.html (accessed 21 December 2014).

context, adding, 'They should be getting that kind of treatment because they should know what to play on national television and what not to play. We play for our country with a lot of passion, and it disappoints all the players sometimes to see what characters they make out of us. If I don't do well on the ground they will show us as *3 Idiots* (a Bollywood flick). Harbhajan is one of the idiots, MS Dhoni is the other. That is not right. I know it sounds funny but it is not.'

Hardly the sort of conduct one expects from a player, it was nevertheless difficult to deny that his outburst pointed towards a vital truth. Cricketers are put through countless trials by the media. The ones who have good track records are expected to do well, day after day, in every match and tournament. A few failures and they find themselves under excessive pressure. The difference between a player and a player who leads the side is an important one though. In any list of two players, the second person is always the captain: especially when the going is bad. The job is not enviably glamorous as people tend to perceive.

Having learned to accept praise and brickbats without losing his cool like Bhajji did, Dhoni led the side in the three-match ODI series which saw India win by 2-1. This series belonged to Tendulkar, who became the first batsman ever to score a double century which he did in the second ODI in Gwalior after India had won the first tie. Along with Dhoni, he added 101 runs in 8.5 overs and reached the elusive mark of 200 not out in the last over. Dhoni was on a rampage, scoring an unbeaten 68 off 25 deliveries as India reached 401 for 3. The South Africans struggled to chase that down and eventually fell short by 153 runs. In the third ODI, the tourists won as India tested their bench strength. The experiment backfired, which was acceptable to the cricket fans as long as their team won the series, which they did.

The IPL followed, and this time Dhoni led his team to their first title. He would follow that sometime later with another title win as the skipper of CSK in the Champions League. After the IPL, but well before the Champions League took place, the Indian team left for the West Indies for the World Twenty20. The initial stage saw India beat Afghanistan and also South Africa, but in the Super Eight stage, they suffered three losses against Australia, West Indies and Sri Lanka.

With voices becoming loud enough to be heard, Dhoni had a thing or two to worry about. His strategies, which included possibly inaccurate decisions about who should have been sent out to bat and when, were being questioned. Criticisms from former cricketers such as Ravi Shastri and Anil Kumble appeared in the media. However, such is the schedule of Indian cricket that the team needed to move on. Having won the Asia Cup for the last time way back in 1995, the Indian team was hoping to set the record straight by getting it right—and bringing the title home—this time around.

Before reaching the finals for a faceoff with Sri Lanka, India had to confront their share of roadblocks. They beat Pakistan by three wickets in a last over finish along the way, with Dhoni contributing an absolutely crucial half-century in the team's effort. In the league stage, Sri Lanka went past them. In the finals, India won, and that too by a massive margin of 81 runs. After a gap of fifteen years, the Cup was finally theirs.

TWIST IN THE TALE

INDIA BROADLY HAS two kinds of celebrities: film stars and cricketers. Some are from other categories, among them Sania Mirza in tennis, Saina Nehwal in badminton and Mary Kom in boxing. But no other discipline except the Hindi film industry can be compared to cricket which, as the tired but apt cliche goes, is a religion in our country.

Dhoni's status of a cricketing megastar was reason enough to track him down wherever he went out during his days as a bachelor. Entertainment supplements and television news capsules talked about his alleged affairs with film stars such as Deepika Padukone, Lakshmi Rai and Asin. This writer met a former friend of his who chooses to remain unnamed while divulging a 'dramatic truth.' What was this truth? Mahi had told him about his fondness for Deepika during one of his visits to Ranchi.

'Boss, let me tell you what happened. You can write about it. But don't mention my name,' he requested. After repeated assurances, he took off. 'One day, Mahi and I were sitting in his house. Chachi (Dhoni's mother) was close by. There was an advertisement on the television which had Deepika in it.' He went on and on, 'When I saw it, I called Chachi and asked how she would respond if the actor became her daughter-in-law. Chachi said that Mahi's marriage was his own decision and she would accept the girl who he believes will make a good wife for him.' Although there was nobody around, this friend who was sharing a 'big story' started talking in barely audible whispers. 'I asked Mahi about his friendship with Deepika later. He said he liked her, and it seemed she liked him too. He just didn't know how to take it forward.'

The fellow in Ranchi was as trustworthy—or untrustworthy—as the majority of news items published in the widely read gossip columns in newspapers and magazines. Interestingly, nobody had been able to get a lot of information about Sakshi Singh Rawat, the girl whom Dhoni had been dating in secret for a while.

The Indian captain is said to have met Sakshi at a party hosted by Hindi film actor Bipasha Basu to celebrate the success of *Raaz*, her latest release then. At that time, Sakshi, who studied at the Institute of Hotel Management in Aurangabad, had been working as a front desk personnel at the Taj Bengal, Kolkata. In 2009, stories spread that the Indian captain had been seen with her in Mussoorie. Sakshi apparently closed all her social networking accounts thereafter. That she was a private person contributed to the process of ensuring that their affair didn't turn into a daily news item.

How Dhoni managed to keep the news of his engagement a well-guarded secret is a puzzle. But after the news leaked, the media went on a treasure hunt for exclusive photographs and news reports. *The Times of India* reported, 'The Dhonis played the typical hide and seek on the night of the engagement as the news leaked and the frenzy began to build up. The ceremony took place in Component Palace Hotel, Selaqui, an industrial hub 20 kilometres away from Dehradun. Officials from the hotel informed, "Dhoni and his family flew from Ranchi to Doon airport. They had booked the hotel on July 2 and checked in on July 3, at 6 am. The engagement was supposed to take place in the hotel at night. But at the last minute, they shifted the venue to Bhagirath Resort."[45] The marriage took place at the Vishranti Resort at Bidhauli, which is situated at a distance of 25 kms from Dehradun. Among those who were said to have been invited were some local politicians and his cricketer friends Harbhajan Singh, Ashish Nehra, R P Singh, Suresh Raina and Rohit Sharma. Also present was the owner of Chennai Super Kings and the then BCCI Secretary, N Srinivasan.

Film star Bipasha Basu was there and so was her then-boyfriend John Abraham, Dhoni's close friend. Within a day or two, Bipasha was flooded with calls from the media which wanted to know the details of a so-called party which John and she were hosting for the newly-married Dhoni in Mumbai. Clueless about the so-called party that people were talking about, Bipasha was naturally flabbergasted.

Dehradun being the city where all the action took place, Ranchi missed out on a lot of excitement. Mediapersons did what was expected of them. They went to his residence in Harmu Colony and pestered the guard to reveal the story of the girl who had cast a spell on the Indian skipper. The hassled guard claimed that he knew nothing apart from the fact that Dhoni's parents had gone out of town. While efforts to get

---

[45]'Chat mangni pat byah', *The Times of India*, Devanshi Seth and Piyali Dasgupta, 5 July 2010. http://timesofindia.indiatimes.com/ entertainment/hindi/bollywood/news/Chat-mangni-pat-byah-for-MS-Dhoni/articleshow/6127518.cms (accessed 21 December 2014).

some information didn't stop right away, the cricketer's fans started celebrating in Ranchi. They burst firecrackers, distibuted sweetmeats and enjoyed the thought that the boy from their town had got married. Kolkata, too, enjoyed since Dhoni's in-laws owned a flat in Alipore. Dhoni used to visit the place, but nobody in the neighbourhood knew about his plans to get married to Sakshi.

After the wedding took place, Lakshmi Rai, who featured in the list of Dhoni's 'friends'—a word used smartly to suggest a relationship in gossip columns—finally revealed to *The Times of India*, 'Whenever I was asked about my relationship with Dhoni I said we were just friends and that he would announce his engagement or marriage with someone else soon enough… I knew he was seeing Sakshi, but being a close friend of his, I had to keep it under wraps, because he did not wish to talk about it at the time.'[46]

Dhoni had been so discreet that almost of his teammates had no idea of the development. This included Yuvraj Singh, who tweeted, 'Got to know Mahi is getting married! Congratulations Dhoni and Sakshi. Hope u have a great life together. God bless!! Yuvi and family.' 'How r u guys, my heartiest congratulations to Dhoni,' Tendulkar, who may not have been able to attend the event, tweeted. Legendary singer Asha Bhonsle wrote on her twitter page, 'Heard news that Dhoni got engaged. Best wishes to him.'

Dhoni's marriage was an intensely private affair, unlike his cricket which was in full public view and had made him what he was.

---

[46]'I'm out of it now: Friend', *The Times of India*, 5 July 2010. http://timesofindia.indiatimes.com/india/Im-out-of-it-now-Friend/ articleshow/6129266.cms (accessed 21 December 2014).

BACK IN THE GAME

SOON AFTER THE change in his personal life, Dhoni was on the move again with India going to Sri Lanka for a three-Test series. They lost the first one at Galle by ten wickets and drew the second in Colombo in a high-scoring match. But the team drew level by winning the third tie in Colombo by five wickets. This was made possible by a brilliant century by Laxman, who remained unbeaten on 103 while battling a back pain. After the match ended, the skipper couldn't stop praising his special batsman and expressed hope that he will continue to play knocks like that in future.

Three days after the Test series had ended, an ODI tri-series featuring India, New Zealand and hosts Sri Lanka began. In the India–New Zealand tie, the latter not only defeated the former, but annihilated them. Batting first, New Zealand put up 288 on the board and skittled out India for 88 runs later, with Jadeja, who emerged as the highest scorer getting 20 of them. Losing by 200 runs was embarrassing for India.

To India's credit, they got their act together and reached the finals in which Sri Lanka walked all over them and won by 74 runs. In numerical terms, Dhoni's 67 was his best in the series. But he took 100 balls to get there. He couldn't have done much, since he kept on losing partners while batting.

The skipper was the last man to get out without being able to pull off a miracle with his dexterous finishing abilities.

As a team leader on the field, he did just fine. What he correctly pointed out after the loss was that his batsmen were unable to share partnerships of consequence, and also that the bowlers did bowl wide in the initial stages which didn't help even though the conditions helped them. The ICC World Cup wasn't far away, and the members of Team India under Dhoni needed to pull up their socks really fast.

The Champions League was an intervention. After it ended, Dhoni would have been a happy man with CSK having won the title, which meant he had led the team to triumphs in both the IPL and the Champions League in the same year.

Now it was time to face the Aussies.

Laxman loved the Aussies. When he got going, watching him bat was one of the most sublime sights in world cricket. Chasing 216 for victory in Mohali, the Indian team stumbled and fumbled. In came VVS, whose back pain was threatening to play spoilsport. He conquered his handicap and, in the company of Ishant Sharma, scored an extraodinary 73 not out to guide India to a thrilling one-wicket win.

India strolled to an easy seven-wicket win in Bangalore. This match was a Tendulkar show, with the master getting 214 in the first innings and remaining unbeaten on 53 in the second. Talking about the pressure on players, which didn't reflect in the verdict, Dhoni said, 'One good thing in both the Test matches, even though the last-innings targets were not huge, was that there was pressure on both the sides. Ultimately it was a close finish in both the games. You may look at this scorecard and say this was an easy win, but still there was nervousness in the dressing room. I think it was a good short Test series we had.' Because of heavy rains, only one out of three ODI matches was completed. It was played at Vishakapatnam, and India won. The Ricky Ponting-led Australian team took the plane back without a single win.

After the Australians left, the New Zealanders toured India towards the end of the year. The first two Tests at Ahmedabad and Hyderabad ended in draws. At Nagpur, Dravid led the way to score 191 while Dhoni, whose batting form had been poor lately, scored a fine 98. India scored 566 in their first and only innings as the visitors collapsed to an innings defeat.

An ODI series in which Gambhir captained the side would follow. But even after the easy victory in Nagpur, the Indian skipper was already thinking ahead. 'There are plenty of players who have toured South Africa before, so gaining information from them will be really important. But it will be a team effort. And as a team, we will have to do the basics right.' The presence of some talented youngsters notwithstanding, India was clearly banking on experience during the tough tour to South Africa. The message was loud and clear.

Dhoni skipped the ODI series which the hosts won 5-0 under Gambhir's leadership, but came back for India's tough one: the tour to South Africa. The Indians were hammered by an innings and 25 runs in Centurion. Dhoni with his 33 and 90 batted well, while Tendulkar made an unbeaten 111 in the second innings. But India's bowling, which had allowed the hosts to score 620 for 4 declared in their only innings, had the captain worried. Talking to the media, he admitted that his bowling, which allowed South Africa to score 620 for 4 in their only innings, was an area of concern.

Durban was a seriously low-scoring affair, but Laxman sparkled amidst the fall of wickets on both sides to score 96 which sealed an 87-run win for India. The third Test in Cape Town produced a draw, which implied that Dhoni hadn't lost a single Test series as the leader of the Indian team. India had their chances in Cape Town. Dhoni admitted to that only after the match was over. On the whole, however, the Indian skipper had every reason to be satisfied since the team returned with a 1-1 verdict against a very tough side in their opponent's home turf.

The year had ended with India holding to the number one spot in the ICC Test rankings. Dhoni had led the CSK to title wins in the IPL and the Champions League in South Africa. He had married his girlfriend Sakshi. All in all, it had been a good year.

What will happen in the World Cup that was scheduled to be played in India, Sri Lanka and Bangladesh in 2011? Even before the tournament had begun, Dhoni probably knew that every Indian fan was somehow convinced that he and his team would win.

It was a great expectation, and one that had to be met. Somehow.

PEAK AND DESCENT

THE INDIAN TEAM'S triumph at the Prudential World Cup
in 1983 was a miracle of destiny. But, 2011 offered a different
set of challenges. Having led the team to several memorable
victories, India under its unflappable skipper was expected to
win in familiar conditions. Since 1975, when England had
played host to the inaugural edition of the World Cup, no
team had been able to win the tournament on home soil.
History, thus, posed an intimidating challenge to the Indian
team before its campaign in the most prestigious cricket
tournament actually began.

In 2003, India, under the leadership of Ganguly, had
performed admirably to reach the finals. Australia, a powerhouse
of seemingly limitless talent at that time, beat them in the
finals. That memory hurt. In 2007, India had been humiliated
by Bangladesh and sent back home before the Super Eights.
The year 2011, therefore, was seen as a godsend that India
was supposed to exploit. As time went by and the tournament
came nearer, public pressure intensified. It was tough.

The ICC World Cup in 2011 incorporated a significant
change in the manner in which the teams were grouped. Two
associate nations were dropped, bringing down the number of
teams to 14 instead of 16 as seen in 2007. Unlike the earlier

format in which the teams were divided into four groups of four, 2011 had two groups of seven, which implied that each team had to play in six matches.

The tournament, which began on 19 February, was scheduled to end with the finals on 2 April.

India's match against Bangladesh was the first of the tournament. Will history repeat itself? It did not, as Dhoni's men cruised to an 87-run win at Mirpur. Sehwag scored a 140-ball 175 while young Kohli, playing in his first World Cup, raced to an unbeaten 100. The skipper remained padded up inside the pavilion as India reached a huge total of 370 for 4. The top-and middle-order of Bangladesh fought hard, but a target of 371 never seemed to be within their reach for a moment. However, had every Indian bowler gone berserk like Sreesanth, the story might have been different. Never in control over his line and length, Sreesanth gave away 53 runs in his 5 overs.

After a gap of eight days, India met England at Bangalore. This was 'the' match that the mega-tournament was looking for. Although the verdict—the first tie for both the teams in their respective World Cup histories—was a dissatisfying outcome for both India and England, it showed that the tournament didn't have any clear cut favourite. India in subcontinental conditions was a very strong outfit, but India's bowling was a huge worry. A couple of bad days with the bat and they could be in serious trouble: this message acted as a dampener for the fans of Indian cricket.

That Harbhajan bowled the least expensive spell, conceding 58 runs in his 10 overs, showed just how badly India's bowling was massacred. When England reached 281 for 2 after 42.4 overs, the match seemed as good as lost. That is when Zaheer

Khan sent Ian Bell (69), Strauss and Paul Collingwood (1) back. The tourists needed 29 from 3 overs, which would have been tough to get had the erratic leggie Chawla not given away 15 runs in the 49th overs. Dhoni asked Munaf Patel to bowl the last over. With two runs to get from the last ball, the match could have swung either way. Graeme Swann struck the ball really hard, but it was stopped at mid off, resulting in a single and a tie.

Yuvraj Singh supported by Khan and Pathan ensured that India won their tie against Ireland at Bangalore rather easily. First, Yuvi rolled his arm over to pick up five Irish wickets for 31 to limit the opposition's total to 207. When Dhoni got out for 30, India at 167 for 5 didn't look entirely comfortable. But the left hander kept his cool to score an unbeaten 50. Pathan's pyrotechnics, which took him to 30 not out from 24 balls, took India home with 24 balls and 5 wickets to spare.

India's win against the Netherlands in Delhi was a walkover. Although the Dutch were bundled out for 189 and the home team went past the target in 36.3 overs, Yuvraj with an unbeaten half century and Dhoni with a 19 not out had to make sure that India did not face any more scare after five wickets had gone with the score reading 139. The next match in Nagpur against the mighty South Africans was an important one. Will India win or lose? The question was a worrying one, and no fan of Indian cricket wanted to believe that a depressing answer was on the way. But the sad part for them was, Dhoni and his men were defeated by three wickets in spite of scoring a reasonably respectable 296 (all out) anchored by a Tendulkar century and a fantastic opening stand of 142 shared between Tendulkar and Sehwag (73). Gambhir at number three scored 69. But the last nine batsmen were sent back home after adding 29 runs, while Dhoni (12 not out) stood at the other end and watched.

India's win against the Windies in Chennai by 80 runs was a one-sided affair. Yuvraj with a century and two opposition wickets was the star of the match once again. Then came what is known as a crunch game against the Australians in Ahmedabad in the quarter finals. Although India won the match by five wickets and 14 balls to spare, one might justifiably wonder what might have happened had Yuvraj not scored his unbeaten half century and bowled an economical spell (2/44) once again. Although Tendulkar and Gambhir scored 50s too, the young left hander was at his best. Dhoni on his part went back after scoring seven. But the manner in which he marshalled his limited bowling resources was worth watching.

The law of averages caught up with Yuvraj when he went back after scoring a duck against Pakistan in the semi-finals at Mohali. But Tendulkar had a fine outing, scoring 85 as India scored 260 for 9. Pakistan in response was all out for 231 as all the five Indian bowlers picked up two wickets each. It was a battle that every Indian fan wanted their home team to win very badly, and that had happened. For some, this win against Pakistan was as good as winning the finals. Well almost. But the fact was, the verdict resulted in the all-important tie against Sri Lanka at the Wankhede Stadium in Mumbai on 2 April, the verdict that would decide which nation will keep the Cup.

India won, despite Mahela Jayawardene scoring a brilliant 103 not out to take his team to 274 for 6. India's beginning was terrible, with Lasith Malinga sending back Sehwag and Tendulkar with the score still at 31. After that, Gambhir and Kohli shared an 83-run partnership before the latter was dismissed for 35. The score at 114 for 3 sounded more respectable than before, but the target of 275 was far away. This was the time when Dhoni made a sudden move which took everybody by surprise. His form with the bat had been ordinary in the tournament. But he promoted himself ahead of Yuvraj. This decision proved to be the turning point of the match.

Gambhir had been playing a polished knock at the other end. But Dhoni counter-attacked. He took on the Sri Lankan bowling with Gambhir, who provided fantastic support before losing his wicket on 97. Yuvraj, who came out next, remained not out on 21 while Dhoni who scored a 79-ball 91 hit the winning runs: a six off the bowling of Nuwan Kulasekara. India won by six wickets with 10 balls to spare. If Yuvraj won the Man of the Tournament award, Dhoni had won the Man of the Match in the finals. After Kapil Dev's men's surprise win in 1983, the Indian team under MS Dhoni had made the trophy theirs.

Talking about his decision to promote himself ahead of Yuvraj, *The Telegraph*, London noted, 'Cricket folklore is littered with game-changing decisions, but Dhoni's promotion of himself to No 5, after a mediocre run with the bat, will become the stuff of legend. There were sound cricketing decisions for having a right-hander to combat the turn all three of Sri Lanka's off-spinners were getting, but to promote yourself ahead of Yuvraj Singh, the man of the tournament, takes chutzpah as well as self-belief, characteristics which shaped the innings that followed.'[47]

---

[47]'Cricket World Cup 2011: bold move from India captain Mahendra Singh Dhoni is already the stuff of legend', *The Telegraph*, 3 April 2011. http://www.telegraph.co.uk/sport/cricket/cricket-world-cup/8425142/Cricket-World-Cup-2011-bold-move-from-India-captain-Mahendra-Singh-Dhoni-is-already-the-stuff-of-legend.html (accessed 22 December 2014).

Former Australian skipper Ian Chappell ranked him among the best contemporary leaders in Cricinfo magazine. Chappell wrote, 'India's emphatic victory in the World Cup has proved beyond doubt they are currently the best all-round cricket team. In the process, Mahendra Singh Dhoni's polished performance as skipper, where he pushed, prodded and cajoled his side into peaking at the right time, has shown he's not only the best leader in the game but also one of the finest of the last 30 years. His performance ranks him with the other top-class leaders of the period: Imran Khan, Mark Taylor and Arjuna Ranatunga.'[48]

If the nation went crazy after the World Cup, the media quite justifiably wrote numerous articles praising the Indian skipper. *The Hindu* said, 'Ahead of the World Cup, widely perceived as the most open in recent times, India found itself in an unenviable position: anointed as the favourite and appointed to play in front of volatile, demanding home crowds. A measure of the constricting pressure India's cricketers experienced during the tournament may be had from captain M.S. Dhoni's revelation that his men struggled to keep their food down and that Yuvraj Singh was physically sick because of anxiety.' It added, 'Seen in this light, India's second World Cup triumph—28 years after the gloriously improbable victory Kapil Dev's team achieved against the mighty West Indies—appears all the more remarkable.'[49]

---

[48]'Dhoni's among the great modern captains', *Cricinfo*, 10 April 2011. http://www.espncricinfo.com/magazine/content/story/510271.html (accessed 22 December 2014).
[49]'Behind India's World Cup', *The Hindu*, 3 April 2011. http:// www.thehindu.com/opinion/editorial/behind-indias-world-cup/ article1597036.ece (accessed 22 December 2014).

This was not a time for too much criticism, and an article in ESPNcricinfo.com reflected that approach. 'A daunting batting line-up—Sachin Tendulkar, Virender Sehwag MS Dhoni et al.—a vastly improved fielding unit and an attack boasting variation and control provided the basis of India's second World Cup success. They became the first host nation to lift the trophy and, after several years of planning and building, developed what their influential coach, Gary Kirsten, referred to as "a sense of destiny" about their triumph.'

Although Tendulkar had contributed very little in the finals, just 18 in fact, his teammates hoisted him on their shoulders. After years of serving Indian cricket, this was that one triumph which had eluded him. Dhoni almost dodged the limelight as the focus shifted to the Master Blaster, who travelled for a while on the shoulders of his teammates. If there was anybody who deserved to have all the focus on him, it was Tendulkar and not Dhoni. What the Indian skipper did before the win was what had scripted this victory. India were a very good side but certainly not unbeatable. His players had been under pressure all through. So, he chose to attend most of the press conferences and took on questions from the media. He displayed exemplary restraint on the field and encouraged his players without losing his famous calm ever. He shocked most in the finals by batting ahead of Yuvraj, and what a fantastic decision it turned out to be.

It was during his first one-on-one interview to CNN-IBN that he expressed his innermost feelings. 'It was one of the biggest things for us as Indian cricketers, you know. We are playing at the top level. We all want to be part of a World Cup-winning side. The last time we won the proper 50-over version was 28 years back. So most of the people [in the] side wanted to win the World Cup, and as soon as we got into a position where we saw the World Cup coming into our dressing room, emotions started to flow. If you see, before the post match presentation, almost every player cried...'

Did he cry? He confessed, 'Yes, I did. You don't have footage of that.' He added, 'It's very difficult to control an emotion like that. I was controlling [myself]. I wanted to quickly go up to the dressing room, and I saw two of my players crying and running to me. All of a sudden, I started crying, and I looked up and there was a huddle around me. It just so happened that you don't have footage of it—you just see me coming up and doing that. And each and every one cried.'[50]

After the World Cup triumph, the Indian players hardly got any breathing space, which they richly deserved. Understandable, since the IPL's fourth edition began barely one week later. Chennai Super Kings had won the previous edition. So, the big question was: will they repeat the act which nobody else had? They did, which surprised very few since he was being seen as a captain who couldn't put a foot wrong. In spite of CSK becoming the first team to win back-to-back IPL titles, Dhoni along with some other leading players skipped India's ODI series in the West Indies. Led by a young Raina, the inexperienced team still managed to beat the hosts 3-2 without too many difficulties.

For the Test series, India were back to his usual strength. Led by Dhoni, the team met the West Indies in the first Test at Kingston, Jamaica. In a low-scoring affair, India won the match by 63 runs. Two performances stood out in the Test:

[50]'I love to be in the moment: Dhoni', IBNLive, 17 December 2011.

Rahul Dravid's century and debutant medium pacer Praveen Kumar's performance with the ball which allowed him to pick up six crucial wickets. What was terrible about this match was an episode whose protagonists were Dhoni and umpire Daryl Harper.

Harper was supposed to retire after the last Test of the series. Reporting on a now-notorious incident, Wisden reported, 'The Indians were openly distrustful of umpire Harper's decisions, eventually prompting his withdrawal from the final Test, which had been scheduled to be his last. Dhoni told the post match media conference that 'if the correct decisions were made, the game would have finished much earlier, and we would be in the hotel by now'. Harper claimed that the Indian captain badgered him on the field, saying: 'We've had issues with you before, Daryl.'

The report added, 'Harper said he chose to retire prematurely because of the Indians' pressure on him. He left with sharp criticism not only of the Indians ("I should never have applied the laws of cricket to Indian players") but also of what he termed the ICC's failure to take action against Dhoni, and its lack of support for him.'[51] The Harper controversy left a bad taste in the mouth of every cricket lover.

The second Test at Bridgetown ended in a draw, but not before Dhoni had taken a brave decision to set 280 to win in 77 overs. The Windies struggled to reach 202 in 71.3 overs before bad light forced the umpires to call off the match because of poor light. The third Test at Dominica was marked

---

[51]'West Indies v India in West Indies, 2011', *Wisden*, Tony Cozier. http://m.espncricinfo.com/page2/content/story/589101.html (accessed 22 December 2014).

by Dhoni's 74 in the first innings, his only decent knock in what had been a pathetic series with the bat otherwise. In the second innings, in what seemed like a desperate decision to save the match and win the series, Dhoni and Laxman left the field when India needed 86 runs from the remaining 15 overs. Later, it transpired that Dhoni and the West Indies skipper Darren Sammy had decided to call the match off. India's decision not to chase down the target was a pathetic decision, which called for widespread criticism in the cricketing circles. In hindsight, Dhoni should have gone for the target. His decisions to act otherwise found hardly any takers.

Soon came the Pataudi Trophy between India at England which began on the 21 June, 2011 and carried on till 22 August, at the Lord's. As India would learn soon, this series was going to be an absolute disaster.

The Lord's Test was the 2000th in the history of international cricket. Not only that, it was the 100th played between India and England in which the former went down by 196 runs. That hurt. In the second Test at Trent Bridge, India did earn a first innings lead of 67 runs, thanks to another Rahul Dravid century. But England hit back with 544 runs. Faced with a target of 478 in the second innings, India went to pieces and lost the match by 319 runs. Dhoni's misery with the bat continued, with his scores of 5 and a first-ball duck doing nothing to contribute to the cause of the Indian team's performance.

At Edgbaston, Dhoni recovered some of his batting form, scoring 74 in the first innings and 77 not out in the second. But such scores came to nothing as Alastair Cook went on a rampage to make 294. The hosts won by an innings and 242 runs. Three-nil down in a four-Test series, here was a team that was completely down and out. At The Oval, England propelled by Bell's 235 and Pietersen's 175 gave India a parting gift it couldn't have asked for: a defeat by an innings and 8 runs. Since their defeat against Australia way back in 1968, India had lost 4-0 in a four-Test series for the first time ever.

With India dead and buried in a cricketing disaster of the kind none would have anticipated before the tour began, *Cricinfo* magazine asked, 'Exaggeration aside, this series has suspended our sense of reality. Have England really become awe-inspiringly good, or has India's awfulness made them look so? Conversely, have India, undefeated in a Test series since August 2008 before this, become utterly appalling in a matter of months, or have England dragged them there with the force of their performances?'[52]

Having been whitewashed as badly as one could have imagined, Dhoni still retained his composure during the press conference. When asked whether he felt any decline in enthusiasm during the course of this forgettable series, he said, 'I don't believe in surrendering. This job was given to me when I didn't really expect it and I'm not a person that believes in surrendering. I'm giving it my best shot and that's what it's all about.' This was his first series defeat after taking over as the skipper. A young boy of yesteryears was learning to grow.

If Rahul Dravid's superb performance with the bat was the only consolation from the Test series, Dhoni's Man of the Series performance in the ODI series that India lost 3-0 was the solitary comfort for a man who came back home, disheartened and routed. That the only Twenty20 match led

---

[52]'Are England great or India wretched?', *Cricinfo*, Sambit Bal, 22 August 2011. http://www.espncricinfo.com/magazine/content/story/528963. html (accessed 22 December 2014).

to a six-wicket loss didn't help matters either.

An ouster from the group stage in the Champions League followed. Not much later, England came down to India to play in a five-match ODI series. India won 5-0 this time. But the defeat didn't compensate for the humiliation suffered by the Indian team not very long ago. Dhoni won another Man of the Series award for his performances with the bat, his two standout shows being a knock of 87 not out in the first match at Hyderabad which also won him the Man of the Match award and another of 75 not out in the last fixture at the Eden Gardens in Kolkata where the Man of the Match award was picked up by young all-rounder Ravindra Jadeja for his spell of 4/33.

In November 2011, the West Indies came visiting to play in a three-Test series which India won 2-0. Dhoni played just one knock of any substance, but that turned out to be an aggressive 144 from 175 balls with ten fours and five sixes in the second Test in Kolkata. Although VVS Laxman's pivotal innings of 176 not out set up the win by an innings and 15 runs, it was Dhoni's knock which demoralised the West Indies so badly that they failed to make any impact on the Test match. The third Test in Mumbai ended with India needing 1 run to win with one wicket in hand when the team ran out of overs to bat.

In the history of Test matches, this was the second time that a Test match had ended in a draw with the scores level after the fourth innings, the first time being the England–Zimbabwe tie at Bulawayo in 1996-97. For every cricket lover, this was a match to remember.

Dhoni did not play in the ODI series against the West Indies thereafter, which India won 4-1. This series will be best remembered for Sehwag's fireworks as he raced to 219, the new record in ODI cricket. The series ended on a winning note before India left for Australia with a solitary aim in mind: that of winning the first ever series 'Down Under.' Under Michael Clarke, the Australian team which was experiencing a transition had lost to South Africa and New Zealand. In spite of the disaster in England, everybody was expecting India to win, especially those who believed that Indians weren't 'bad travellers' any longer as they were once called.

Every supporter was stung by a reality bite after the first Test at Melbourne which India lost by 122 runs. Sehwag, Dravid and Tendulkar batted well in the first innings although India's score of 282 fell short of Australia's 333 because of a lower order collapse. Facing a target of 292 in the second innings, India was skittled out for 169.

The year 2012 began with India's defeat by an innings and 68 runs in Sydney. In the first innings, only Dhoni went past the 50-run mark as India was bundled out for 169. Australia declared their first innings at 659 for 4 with Clarke scoring an unbeaten 329 and Ponting (134) and Michael Hussey (150) supporting him brilliantly. Although Gambhir, Tendulkar, Laxman and Ashwin scored half-centuries, with the first two getting out only in their 80s, India managed to score 400 which was a good total, but far from being enough. After two matches, they were 2-0 down.

Before the third Test in Perth began, it was clear where the Border–Gavaskar Trophy would stay. What was not clear was whether India would suffer another innings defeat, which it did. The margin, that of an innings and 37 runs, couldn't have been bettered since the team had just about managed to reach 161 and 171 in their two innings this time.

After the series ended, Dhoni, instead of shying away, took it on the chin. 'I am the leader of the side. I am the main culprit so of course I blame myself.' He added,'As far as the amount of cricket that I have seen this is definitely one of the worst phases where we have not done well consistently...Again I am repeating myself, four Tests in England, three Tests here, we have not put runs on the board.' Injuries in the bowling department were a big setback as well, he said. What was remarkable was that he didn't try to pass the buck and blame his colleagues. He went on to criticise his flop show with the bat as well. Even the biggest Dhoni cynic had to admit that the man's honesty without resorting to escapism deserved respect, not condemnation. India lost the Test at Adelaide too, leading to a strange and shameful situation in which the team had touched an all-time low with eight consecutive away defeats.

With the team having lost so many matches on the trot and public and media scrutiny having become an inseparable part of their lives, Dhoni was leading a fractured unit for sure. Having averaged 20.40 in the Test series, he hadn't been a star performer by the most lenient yardstick of judgment. Seniors appeared to have turned into pale shadows of their once-glorious selves. The Sehwag v/s Dhoni duel arising out of conflicting statements made by the two during this period had added to the tension within the dressing room. Amidst all this stress and disgrace, one young man was coming into his own slowly. His name was Virat Kohli.

One consolation for Team India was that they managed to draw the Twenty20 series against Australia 1-1. Dhoni batted well in both, showing that rising above mediocrity in the shorter version was not a problem for him. This was followed by the CB tri-series featuring Australia, India and Sri Lanka.

India began the first match with a 65-run loss against Australia. But hit back by defeating Sri Lanka by four wickets in their second outing. In Adelaide, they went past Australia by four wickets with two balls to spare in a tense finish. Although Gambhir made a solid 92, Dhoni with his clever batting got a six, two and three off the second, third and fourth deliveries to remain not out on a sedate 44 otherwise.

The next match against Sri Lanka ended in a tie and, once again, it was Dhoni with his 58 not out who chaperoned India to that possibility. But India's encounter against Australia proved to be an absolute disaster. Although Dhoni top-scored with an unbeaten 56, the team crashed to a 110-run defeat. In his absence, Sehwag led the following match against the Sri Lankans which India lost by 51 runs.

After losing to Australia, India had to win against Sri Lanka and they had to win big. Not only that, they had to keep their fingers crossed and hope that Australia would beat Sri Lanka in the last qualifying match. Batting first, Sri Lanka flew to a score of 320 in their quota of 50 overs. This meant that India had to chase down the target of 321 in 40 overs to stay alive in this tournament.

India did, and the star was Virat Kohli, who blasted the Lankan attack to every part of the ground to score 133 not out from 86 balls. India reached 321 in 36.4 overs, which was nothing short of incredible since the team had lost only three wickets while chasing down the target in such a short time. That Australia lost the last qualifier by 9 runs ended the series for India, which hadn't been as bad as one had expected it to be. Although Dhoni didn't need to bat in the last tie, his average of 51.25 showed howcrucial he was to the fortunes of his team.

Indian cricket doesn't pause for a second. That showed once more when Asia Cup began on the 13 March 2012. This tournament was preceded by a significant episode in Indian cricket: that of Dravid's retirement. Dravid, who had brought the curtains down on the ODIs and Twenty20 internationals earlier, announced his retirement from all forms of the game in the international arena. After Kumble and Ganguly, this 39-year-old great was the third senior to say goodbye.

Before the Asia Cup began, every Tendulkar fan had been hoping that he would finally score his his 100th international century. Meanwhile, critics were busy writing epitaphs of his career. Faced with criticism, Tendulkar went out and scored a century against Bangladesh at Mirpur. The innings of 114 from 147 balls was painful to watch, and it eventually played a significant role in India's shocking defeat. India went on to beat Pakistan and and Sri Lanka, but failed to qualify for the finals. Dhoni remained not out in all the three innings he batted. Apart from a highest score of 46 not out against Sri Lanka in a match that India won by 50 runs, he didn't get the opportunity to make any significant contribution.

After the fifth edition of the IPL that was marred by the fixing scandal, India landed in Sri Lanka once again. The tour was an easy one for Indians, who seemed to dig the Lankan conditions. This series is best remembered for the emphatic rise of Kohli, who made the most of the batting conditions to hit two centuries and win the Man of the Series award. With just one 50-plus score apart from two knocks in the 30s, Dhoni put up an unexceptional show with the bat. But India cruised through the series, winning it 4-1, the only bottomline that ultimately matters.

India's nightmares in the overseas tours were recent

episodes, and a triumph in an ODI series between India and Sri Lanka on the latter's home soil was not a good enough consolation. Then came the subsequent series against New Zealand in which Dhoni's men drubbed the visitors in the first Test at Hyderabad by an innings and 115 runs. Battered and bruised, New Zealand travelled to Bangalore to face the hosts in the second match. And, they fought really hard, taking a first innings lead of 12 runs. In the second innings, Ashwin bowled his way to another five-wicket haul and the tourists were dismissed for 248, thus setting a target of 261 for India in the final innings of the match. After five wickets went down for 166, Kohli and Dhoni had to stay calm and steer the team out of trouble which they did. India won the match by five wickets and the two-match series 2-0, a verdict that might have eluded them had either of the two got out.

The Twenty20 international series slipped out of India's hands though. While the first match was abandoned without a single ball being bowled, New Zealand managed to win the second at Chennai by one run in a last-ball finish. In spite of losing the more significant Test series, the visitors had something to cheer about after the tour was over.

After this loss, more Twenty20 cricket was on the way in September 2012, a month that was significant for Dhoni since he was also made the captain of the ICC's ODI Team of the Year for the first time ever. But his focus was on Twenty20 matches, the tournament being the ICC World Twenty20 in Sri Lanka. By that time, the cricketing world had started viewing India as the most formidable training ground for Twenty20 cricket.

India began its campaign with an easy victory against Afghanistan. After downing England in their group, they qualified for the Super Eight stage. In the first tie in the best-of-eight stage, Australia hammered the daylights out of India by defeating them with nine wickets in hand. This was followed by the all-important tie against Pakistan which they had to win to be alive in their tournament. This, they did, by beating their opponents by eight wickets.

Pakistan was bowled out for 128, which was too small a total for any reasonably good Twenty20 outfit. Anchored by Virat Kohli's unbeaten 78, India raced to a win by eight wickets. The major turnaround that affected India took place when Pakistan beat Australia by 32 runs, which implied that South Africa was out of the tournament. India, on the other hand, had to beat South Africa by 31 runs to qualify for the knockout stage.

In Twenty20 cricket, winning a match by 31 runs can be daunting, and more so if you bat first after losing the toss and somehow manage to put up 152 for 6 on the board. Apart from Rohit Sharma who gave away 13 runs in his one over, every other Indian bowler fought hard to contain the South Africans and pick up wickets as well. South Africa fell short of the target, but by one run. For the third time in succession, India failed to reach the decisive stages of the World Twenty20.

After the ouster, Dhoni said that he and his team didn't think that the Pakistan–Australia tie 'would impact us so much.' 'We knew that it would affect us but the required margin while winning was too big so we had a problem.' That was his defence. But critics pointed out the loopholes in his tragedy. As ESPNcricinfo.com observed, 'And ultimately, Dhoni can't escape scrutiny. He has been a remarkable leader on many accounts. But some of his selections and tactics on the field have been perplexing. After watching Pakistan bowl 18 overs of spin to neuter Australia, he chose to pick one spinner against a team comfortable with pace; didn't bowl his lead spinner till the 10th over, brought on Rohit Sharma before using his last specialist bowler, and gave away easy singles while defending 121.'[53] Indeed, in the tie against South Africa, the Indian skipper had blundered.

Using Rohit Sharma ahead of Ashwin against South Africa, dropping Sehwag against Australia, failure of openers, too much dependence on Kohli in the middle order, defensive field placements—too many factors had converged at the same time. Dhoni's captaincy had come under the scanner once more, and this time in the shortest version in the more-comfortable playing conditions in Colombo where India had played all their matches. Having slipped into a critical phase in his captaincy, the Indian skipper-wicketkeeper-batsman must have been a worried man.

---

[53]'India and South Africa can only blame themselves', *ESPNcricinfo.com*, Sambit Bal, 2 October 2012. http://www.espncricinfo.com/icc-world-twenty20-2012/content/story/585274.html (accessed 22 December 2014).

UPS, DOWNS, AND A MAJOR TRIUMPH

THE JOB FOR the man at the top is never easy: and more so, in Indian cricket in which the skipper is constantly under scrutiny. Wins are celebrated, but eventually reduced to sidelights as setbacks under any leader are highlighted. In spite of experiencing both for years, Dhoni had been rewriting the facts of his career as a captain with each passing year.

The period between 2013 and mid-2014 was an eventful one for Indian cricket. When the Pakistan team under the leadership of Misbah-ul-Haq came calling, the two teams won one Twenty20I each before Dhoni experienced the discomfort by averaging 203 with the bat while watching his team go down by 1-2 in the ODI series. The only consolation, if one could call it that, was winning the Man of the Match award by scoring 36 in the biting cold of Delhi, when India won, and batsmen from both sides failed to come to terms with the weather and the pitch.

The first Test between England and India must have come as a relief to Dhoni withthe visitors getting mauled by nine wickets. India's highlight in this match was young Cheteshwar Pujara's double-century. By the time the match had ended, everybody was asking the same question. Had India found a replacement for the great Rahul Dravid? The second Test in Mumbai saw a dramatic reversal. Drubbed in the first tie, a miraculously energised England hit back to trounce India by ten wickets as a result of a sensational second innings collapse because of which the home team were bowled out for 142.

On a high, when the teams went to Kolkata, England defeated India by seven wickets. Cook missed his double century by 10 runs, but he guided England to a commanding position from which there was no looking back. Quiet with the bat apart from a 52 in the Indian first innings in Kolkata, Dhoni was run out for 99 in the first innings of the fourth and final Test at Nagpur. Rising star Kohli scored another century, helping India recover after the innings had begun on a shaky note. Importantly, after this drawn Test, India lost one more Test series.

Former Indian skipper and legendary opener Sunil Gavaskar dropped a bombshell on NDTV, a leading news television channel, after the Nagpur draw. Without endeavouring to be diplomatic, he said, 'Till the fourth day of the Nagpur Test, I would have backed Dhoni. Now that Virat has come up with a hundred under trying circumstances where he curbed his natural game, he discovered a good part about himself.' Talking about Kohli, he added, 'He is ready to take on the mantle of Test cricket. That needs to be looked at in a positive manner by everyone concerned, as that is where the future lies.'[54]

---

[54]'Virat Kohli is ready for Test captaincy: Sunil Gavaskar to NDTV', NDTV Sports, 17 December 2012. http://sports.ndtv.com/india-vs-england-2012/news/200822-virat-kohli-is-ready-for-test-captaincy-sunil-gavaskar-to-ndtv (accessed 22 December 2014).

Gavaskar was not the only one who had spoken out against Dhoni. In the heart of hearts, however, most cricket lovers in the country knew that Kohli had miles to go before he could become a permanent leader of the Test side. He was an extremely talented cricketer, but there were serious questions about his temperament. Dhoni, on the other hand, was a calm leader who had brought out the best in his players for years. Replacing him was a suggestion few fans took seriously in 2012.

When India played against the visitors from England in the ODI series, it gave rise to one outcome, not many who followed the game of cricket would have forgotten easily. After three long years, Dhoni's men claimed the number one spot in the ODI rankings after winning the series 3-2. Raina, who has now become a very important component of Team India, picked up the Man of the Series award. Interestingly, Dhoni didn't dwell on his team's return to the number one spot. Having lost the inconsequential fifth match, whose result was facilitated by an Ian Bell century, he said, '(The) series was as tight as the Test series. We should have won this game, maybe we should have batted more sensibly. But it is a young side and it will learn with time. Thankfully, in three games, we didn't have to bowl those death overs. It remains an area of concern.' However, he praised Ishant Sharma, Jadeja's utility and role and an improvement in the quality of fielding. By the time this series had ended, the Indian skipper was already thinking about the next big ODI tournament: the ICC Champions Trophy, which was scheduled to be held in June.

A four-Test series against Australia followed, the first among which was ruled by the skipper himself. Tearing into the Australian attack consisting of competent or better bowlers such as Mitchell Starc, Nathan Lyon, James Pattinson and Peter

Siddle, Dhoni blasted his way to 224 from 265 balls which included six sixes and twenty-four fours. It was, and still is, his highest ever Test score. Kohli scored a ton, but his innings was put to shade by a skipper who was savage, determined and focused. India chased down its target of 50 in the second innings with eight wickets in hand, an easy win which showed the value of a mammoth lead of close to 200 runs in the first outing. The start had been a great one. Dhoni seemed inspired. The big question now was: what next?

Another Indian win, this time by an innings and 135 runs in Nagpur: the answer was symbolic of a renewal of hope in the Indian team. Responding to Australia's mediocre total of 237 in the first innings, India piled up 503, with Pujara getting 204 and Murali Vijay playing a fine hand in which he made 167. In the second innings, Australia was packed off for 131 with Ashwin (5/69) and Jadeja (3/33) not allowing any batsman to settle down. If Dhoni had won the Man of the Match in the first match, it was Pujara's turn this time, both after after having scored a double century each.

In the third Test at Mohali, Australia posted a total of 408. India responded with 499, the stars of the show being newcomer Shikhar Dhawan (187) and Vijay (153). Australia's lacklustre performance resulted in a meagre 223 in the second innings. Faced with a target of 132, India sped home by six wickets. Dhawan's century from 85 balls was the fastest ever by a debutant. Among the completed innings by a debutant, Dhawan's was the highest ever. Records tumbled as he went about getting his runs. The batsman who had made a belated entry into Test cricket had made his mark. Two seniors were dropped: Sehwag, a 104-test-old class act, who seemed to have lost his touch, and Harbhajan, who was replaced by Pragyan

Ojha. Their resting was hardly surprising, since Dhoni didn't hesitate to drop players when they lost their form.

Three-nil up and having won the Border–Gavaskar trophy, India went into the fourth Test that was played in Delhi. After taking a slender lead of 10 runs in the first innings, India wiped out Australia for 164 in the second innings and went past the target of 155 with four wickets down. In a low-scoring affair, young Ravindra Jadeja with his seven-wicket-match haul, including a five-for and a useful 43 in the first innings, won the Man of the Match award. India had made a 4-0 sweep. Other memories from recent history were blurred, for a while at least.

After the triumph, Captain Cool chose to be as relaxed as ever. There was no show of strength, no usage of strong words such as 'revenge' which is what India had achieved after a bad mauling at the hands of the visiting team on its home soil in 2012. Talking to the media, he said, 'It doesn't matter if it's 0-4, 2-2, 2-0, 3-1... I don't like words like revenge coming out of the series because in the very next question people talk about the spirit of the game. So revenge, spirit of the game—the vocabulary becomes too confusing.'

Dhoni backed the coach Duncan Fletcher, who had been having a torrid time and was being significantly blamed for India's failures earlier. 'His technical knowledge of batting is immense. He is there helping all the youngsters who have come into the team to groom them to do well in different conditions. Specially, I am very happy for him because he has only seen and spent tough periods with us....'

While talking to the press, the Indian skipper, who had been a beleaguered man till recently, explained the value of 'good habits' in youngsters. 'I may not be there in two, three, four years' time. But all these cricketers, they will be around for eight to ten years. So it's important that they start off with good habits and continue with them, so when the newer generation comes under them, they also just go ahead with the good habits.' Clearly, here was a skipper who was thinking ahead of his own tenure.

Cricket continued, but the game in India experienced a new twist no cricket lover would have liked. The Indian Premier League season was marred by the spot fixing scandal, which gave rise to an atmosphere of gloom in Indian cricket. Amidst all the tension and drama, the team left for the ICC Champions Trophy in England. This was that one huge stage in which India had to deliver. Everything seemed to be going their way after the team gelled as a unit and reached the semi-finals against Sri Lanka in which the quick bowlers Ishant Sharma, Umesh Yadav and Bhuvneshwar Kumar bowled with such impeccable accuracy that Dhoni was able to set a 7-2 field which is hardly, if ever, seen in an ODI-series match. They unleashed such terror that India contained Sri Lanka to 181 for 8 and Dhoni himself enjoyed the luxury of bowling 4 overs in which he only gave away 17 runs.

The winning skipper called the verdict a 'well-written script,' and explained that he had taken on the responsibility of a bowler since the 'ball was doing a bit' and he wanted to save some overs for fast bowlers in the end. 'I thought even if it goes badly, I'll bowl one over. It went okay so I bowled another,' he said. Whether or not he had made the right move by taking the ball was a decision no one questioned since there was no need for it anyway. Sri Lanka had been crushed. The finals against England beckoned, and Dhoni knew what England was waiting for his men. 'England are a very good side and we have played a lot against them in the last couple of years,' He said. If the script of the semis was a good one, that of the finals threatened to go haywire.

Playing the England side on their home soil was not going to be easy. That rains intervened and reduced a 50-over match into a 20 overs per side affair made it worse. India, batting first, only managed to put up 129 for 7, largely due to a rearguard action from Jadeja, who blasted his way to 33 not out from 25 balls. Dhoni himself was out for a duck. England, in response, tottered their way to 124 for 8, resulting in an India win every fan had been waiting for. The result hadn't come under ideal circumstances. With the team having won, however, the 'how' part of the discussion was eliminated. That was understandable.

Dhoni defended the failure of his batsmen later. 'People talk about getting set, getting used to the pace and then playing the big shots. But that was never the case. Whenever the batsmen felt they were set, they had to come off and we had a break of 15-20 minutes. That never allowed us to gain any kind of momentum or build partnerships which were needed. And that was reflected when the middle order went in to bat. It was the main reason why we ended up scoring less than what we had liked to score.' For a change, he spoke about how he had motivated his team to go out and give it their best. While encouraging the players in the huddle, he had told them that 'God' was not going to save them. If they wanted to win the trophy, they had to 'fight it out'. 'We are the number one-ranked side. So let us show that they will have to fight for these 130-odd runs. So let us not look for any outside help,' he said.

The captain had spoken. The team delivered.

When James Tredwell failed to negotiate the last ball of the 20th over in the finals, the visitors and TV viewers saw a unique sight. For once, the Indian skipper actually let his guard down and started jumping. After the superb win followed by Dhoni's rare moment of expressiveness, he was named the captain of the Team of the Tournament. The ICC website noted, 'Dhoni was named as the captain after he led his side to victory in the final, thus becoming the first captain in the history of the game to lift all the three ICC major trophies— ICC World Twenty20 2007, ICC Cricket World Cup 2011 and ICC Champions Trophy 2013. While Dhoni got little opportunity to show his exploits with the bat, he marshaled his troops outstandingly and he was sharp and agile behind the wickets as he accounted for nine batsmen behind the wickets (five catches and four stumpings).'[55]

Former England players were critical about the home team while acknowledging that Team India's quality and Dhoni's leadership skills were simply superb. Darren Gough tweeted, 'Correct, England choked, but India showed why they were the best team in the tournament, Jadeja and Ashwin were quality, Sharma was lucky.' Never one to hold himself back, Andrew Flintoff's tweet had a special mention of the Indian skipper, 'Well played India, Dhoni captained the second half brilliantly! Ultimately the pressure got to England.' Michael Vaughan's tweet said that although England should have won the match comfortably, the 'best team' won the tournament.'

---

[55]'ICC announces Team of the Tournament', *ICC-Cricket.com*, 24 June 2013. http://www.icc-cricket.com/champions-trophy/news/2013/media-releases/70746/icc-announces-team-of-the-tournament (accessed 22 December 2014).

Back home, Rahul Dravid said that the win was needed to inject a spirit of joy after Indian cricket had been hit by the IPL spot fixing scandal. He reflected, 'I think we needed a good positive story. We needed some cheer in our cricket. We needed some happiness in our cricket.' By winning the ICC Champions Trophy, Dhoni and his men had made India smile.

The West Indies Tri-Nation series was the next stop with the Indian selectors making no changes in the team. India won the tournament, but only just, with one wicket in hand and two balls left in the finals against Sri Lanka. Dhoni changed his bat, hit out against the inexperienced Sharminda Eranga in the final over and took his team home after everything seemed lost in India's attempt to chase down a seriously modest target of 202. As usual, the Indian skipper seemed to relish the pressure, upping the run rate until the newcomer came on to bowl in the last over. The moment that happened, Dhoni went after him and finished the match.

After the match, ESPNcricinfo.com noted, 'This was classic Dhoni. He bides his time until the game reaches a boiling point, plays out the best bowlers, pushes the required rate higher and higher, and then backs himself to win the face-off. Javed Miandad did this often. As did Michael Bevan. Dhoni has turned it into an art form.'[56] Certainly not known to elevate self-praise into an art form, Dhoni took a few moments and spoke about his strength. 'I think I am blessed with a bit of good cricketing sense. I thought 15 runs was something

---

[56]'Dhoni keeps his end-over promise', *ESPNcricinfo.com*, Siddhartha Vaidyanathan, 12 July 2013. http://www.espncricinfo.com/tri-nation-west-indies-2013/content/story/650509.html (accessed 22 December 2014).

that I could look for (in the last over), the reason being the opposition's bowler was not someone who is very experienced.' Captain Cool had returned to the match only for the finals, his injury having forced him to sit out with Kohli leading the team earlier. That handicap notwithstanding—his running between the wickets was far slower—he had delivered the killer punch and set an example for his teammates.

The year 2013 turned out to be an exciting year for one-dayers. Playing against Australia, who came visiting in October for an ODI tour, India first won the only Twenty20 match by six wickets. The highlight was Yuvraj Singh's 35-ball 77 not out. The home team went on to win the ODI series thereafter. Rohit Sharma notched up a rare double hundred in the last match and was adjudged the Man of the Series, while Kohli managed to reach his two centuries from 52 and 61 balls respectively in a series in which going past the 300 mark was usually unsafe. Dhoni did not have much to complain about except that the changing of ODI rules, such as the use of two new balls, had resulted in a situation in which the verdict depended on who bowled less badly. But he did make a fleeting mention of the need for improvement in the bowling department, a problem that team India has had to deal with more often than not in recent years.

The two-match Test series against the West Indian tourists delivered results along predictable lines. Led by Darren Sammy, the team, which seemed to have forgotten the rhythms of calypso cricket, was thrashed 2-0. Played in Kolkata, the first tie, which saw the Test debuts of promising paceman Mohammed Shami and middleorder batsman Rohit Sharma resulted in an Indian win by an innings and 51 runs. Shami picked up nine wickets in the match, while Sharma made a sparkling

111 which won him the Man of the Match award. Ashwin's 124 was a demonstration of his correct technique and calm temperament, which received a lot of justified applause from the commentating fraternity. The second Test in Mumbai was as one-sided if not more. India won by an innings and 126 runs, their first innings total of 495 was too steep for the West Indies, who fell for two sub-200 scores in their two innings.

What was far more important than the formality of India's victory was the retirement of Sachin Tendulkar. For everybody right from his fans to his rivals as well as former teammates, keeping a check on emotions was a difficult experience as he bade goodbye with a speech which won't be forgotten by anybody who had watched and heard him on the last day of his glittering cricketing career. Indian cricket minus him had to be the new reality of the future, and reconciling to that truth wasn't going to be easy.

The story of the ODI series had a predictable end. India won it 2-1, although West Indies did manage to get a consolation win in the second ODI at Visakhapatnam. Dhoni remained not out in all his three outings with just one half century in the match that India lost. All in all, the Indian team handed out a massive drubbing to a team whose class had been reduced to a memory.

Once abroad, however, the Indian team faced its share of troubles—and a lot more—on various occasions. When the team went to South Africa, it experienced two very severe losses in the first two ODIs. With the third match declared a no result followed by a tour match which was abandoned without a ball being bowled, the Indian team got ready to face the music in the two-Test series.

Away from the comfort zone of home soil, India's tour to

South Africa had two Tests. The first, played in Johannesburg, had an incredibly tight finish. The tourists batting first scored a modest 280 which included a Kohli century. The hosts responded with 244. India's second innings total of 421 had another Pujara ton (153), while Kohli got out for 96. South Africa aided by centuries from Faf du Plessis (134) and AB de Villiers (103) finished with 450 for 7, the target of 458 so close and yet so far. Both sides must have been unhappy with the verdict. While the South Africans were within touching distance towards the end, India did fancy their chances as well.

In the second match at Durban, the hosts, who were the clear favourites before the series began, thrashed India by ten wickets. The verdict was facilitated by two well-defined reasons: South Africa's first innings total of 500 in response to India's fairly respectable 334 and the latter's disintegration in the second innings in which they struggled to reach 223 in spite of young Rahane's solid knock of 96. Chasing a measly target of 58, the South Africans were never going to be tested. And, they weren't, as they won the match without losing a single wicket.

The Durban Test was an emotional moment for Jacques Kallis, definitely the greatest all-rounder after Sir Garfield Sobers and a highly respected human being too. After playing top class cricket for 18 long years, he retired from Test matches. Dhoni, in the meantime, wasn't particularly unhappy with the performance of his team, his only major concern being that the bowlers needed to adapt themselves to the dry pitches outside the subcontinent.

Dhoni's belief in his young men could not distract the cricket watcher from the fact that India did find itself at the receiving end in overseas conditions often. The New Zealand narrative was no different. India was crushed at her home soil 4-0 in the ODI series, which had nothing to offer barring an exciting match which ended in a tie. Dhoni and Kohli were the only two batsmen who stood among the ruins, and the Indian skipper did mention that India need to stick to the current lot instead of opting for massive chopping and changing. He also said that the batsmen needed to go out and bat with a positive attitude which could also mean picking up those singles and the manner in which they played their defensive strokes. 'What we have seen is that apart from one game, most of the times we have been behind, we have only been doing the catching-up work. And the run-rate goes too high. The last 25 overs, you can't really look to chase eight or nine an over. That was a setback to some extent,' he admitted. By writing a good personal score sheet—40, 56, 50, 79 not out, 47—he had given enough reasons to inspire his team. When that did not happen, all he could have done is look ahead and find results by trusting his men to deliver.

The first Test was played in Auckland—every Indian cricket lover would have been hoping that India would finally break that overseas jinx and win their first Test in 11 matches. As it turned out, the hosts held their nerves and put it past India in Auckland in spite of an admirable chase by India, who fell short by 40 runs. After suffering their tenth defeat in eleven overseas matches, India went to Wellington and drew the match. After New Zealand were all out for 192, India went on to score 403 with Rahane scoring a restrained 118, Dhawan falling short of a century by 2 runs and Dhoni making a quick 68. New Zealand responded with a mammoth 680, with the skipper getting a triple hundred apart from two tons down the order for B J Watling and Jimmy Neesham. India in the fourth innings had to go past 435, and they did experience some serious worries after losing their third wicket at 54. However, Kohli, who scored an unbeaten 105, and Rohit, who remained not out on 31, took the team to safety.

As a skipper, Dhoni's methods were slammed. Dravid said that Dhoni needed to take more risks than he does and also trust his new bowlers. Ganguly was caustic and severe. 'His (Dhoni's) Test captaincy has been obnoxious. But changing captains now will unsettle the team. His place is not in doubt in Test cricket, but Dhoni needs to set the overseas record right,' he told the television channel Headlines Today, adding, 'If the World Cup was not less than a year away, I would have agreed that Dhoni needed to be removed as captain.'[57] Dhoni's excessive use of somebody like Jadeja, who was essentially good as a bowler and has the ability to contain and the skipper's defensive field placements were seen by many experts as reasons why a Test match in which India frittered away its advantages in crucial moments instead of capitalising on them. Four consecutive series defeats abroad was bad news, and most headlines were being written by Dhoni.

An interesting part of the Dhoni story is that the moment the match shifts to the subcontinent, the focus moves away from him to the team, which is definitely qualified to play in familiar conditions. Since the World Twenty20 was in the subcontinent, India had started out as one of the favourites. Placed in Group 2, the team played its first tie against Pakistan

---

[57]'Dhoni's Test captaincy is obnoxious, says Sourav Ganguly', Headlines Today, 19 February 2014. http://indiatoday.intoday.in/story/ganguly-says-dhonis-test-captaincy-obnoxious/1/344448.html (accessed 22 December 2014).

and won with a convincing margin of seven wickets. Another low-scoring affair against the West Indies led to another easy seven-wicket win with Sharma and Kohli getting half centuries. The only dampener was Jadeja's poor show with the ball. He gave away 48 runs in his four-over spell. But that didn't matter. Against Bangladesh, Dhoni came out to bat at number four and finished the match in a hurry. An eight-wicket win: it was simply too easy.

Spin consumed the Australians, who were skittled out for 86 in the fourth match. In helpful conditions, Dhoni has mastered the craft of tigtening the noose around the batsmen by using spin in the shorter version. This one was no different, with Australian wickets falling in a heap for 86 after India had put up 159 for 7 on the board. Dhoni praised Yuvraj for his fine 43-ball 60. 'I think in the middle period Yuvraj batted really well. He gave himself time. It was an ideal opportunity for him to see through the initial ten to fifteen deliveries and we all know the kind of batting line-up we have. Anyone who eats up the deliveries initially and stays till the end, he makes much more than the balls he faces. That's a big positive for us and overall the whole batting line-up got a bit of batting,' he said. His rival captain, George Bailey, was hugely disappointed, but the damage had been done. After losing by 73 runs, Australia went out of the tournament.

It was in the semi-finals that India faced serious resistance for the first time. South Africa put up a respectable score of 172 for 4 in their innings, which seemed like a tough challenge. All the bowlers except Ashwin, who bowled really well to pick up three wickets for 22 runs, and Jadeja, who conceded 8 runs in his two overs, went for runs. But Virat Kohli played a masterclass by scoring a 44-ball 72 not out and anchored

India's chase as the team went past the total for the loss of four wickets with five balls to spare.

Kohli later shared the gesture of his skipper who was with him on the crease. Although the young star had requested Dhoni to finish the match off the last delivery of the penultimate over, the latter chose to play a defensive stroke instead. During the break between overs, he walked up to him and said that giving an opportunity to score the winning runs was his gift to him since he had batted so wonderfully and there was nothing else he could offer. After he had hit those winning runs, the warmth of the gesture became a lovely memory for the young Kohli.

In the finals, India met Sri Lanka. In spite of a fine 77 from Kohli, India struggled to reach 130 for 4. Sri Lanka went past the score with six wickets in hand. Sri Lanka had bowled according to the plan and India failed to speed up at the right time, resulting in very slow progress in the death overs. After the loss, the Indian skipper conceded, 'The last four overs is a place where we really want to score as many as you can and that was an area where we couldn't capitalise. At the same time you have to give credit to the Sri Lankan bowlers. I think they executed their plans brilliantly. They were looking for wide yorkers and all the balls were perfect wide yorkers. I think they only bowled one wide or something. Other than that they were right on the mark, which made it further more difficult for our batsmen to score freely.' Analyses would follow, and so would many more explanations. A realistic assessment of the situation was that Dhoni had led his team to one more major final. This time, he had ended up on the losing side, which was nothing to be ashamed of.

Although Dhoni had delivered on every possible front,

several overseas Test defeats on the trot was a significant shortcoming in his career graph which tormented him. Hence, when his men went on an England tour in mid-2014, he was probably happy to see the first Test at Nottingham against Cook's side end in a respectable draw. Then came Lord's. And India, finally, won a Test match overseas after a three-year-long patch filled with frustrations and disappointments.

Beginning on 17 July, India, batting first, put up 295, an innings that revolved around a ton by the increasingly reliable Rahane (103). With Bhuvaneshwar Kumar, the medium pacer with more guile than speed, Rahane shared a partnership of 90 that proved to be crucial in the long run.

Kumar captured a six-wicket haul when England responded with 319, helped by an in-form newcomer Gary Ballance who scored 110. India's second innings score of 342—made possible by the contributions of Vijay's 95, Jadeja's quickfire 68 and Kumar's 52—implied that England had to score 323 for a win. In England's second innings, what one got to see was a Dhoni–Ishant Sharma show.

By scoring 68 runs of the 214 required on the morning session of the final day, English batsmen Joe Root and Moeen Ali had done what they could do to frustrate the Indian bowlers. Then came the turning point off the last ball of the morning session. Ishant bowled a short one to Moeen, who had shown his vulnerability to that sort of delivery earlier. The ball took off from an awkward length. Moeen ducked. It hit his glove and flew to Pujara crouching at short leg. The batsman was gone. When the two teams left for lunch, India was in a slightly happier frame of mind.

From there, England could never recover. Ishant bowled fast and short. The old ball reared off the pitch, dismissing an out-of-form Matt Prior, their star batsman Root and Ben Stokes who had been having a horrible run with the bat anyway. By the time Stuart Broad went, Ishant had picked up seven wickets for 74 runs. This spell was vintage Ishant, a very tall bowler with the capability to bowl real quick, who was accustomed to making rare statements of his talent followed by long-term descent into abject mediocrity. He was fast, furious and deadly. When the last English batsman James Anderson was run out, England's score was an ordinary 223. India had won a rare match overseas after three years. It was a victory masterminded by Dhoni with his advice to the bowler and appropriate field setting.

At the press conference after the win, Dhoni said, 'When he first came on to bowl, I asked him to bowl short, and he turned the other way. Then I set the field for him so that he couldn't even think of bowling up. So the strategy was to give him a field so he is forced to bowl the length that I wanted him to bowl.' He added, 'It worked, and once he got Moeen's wicket he was eager enough to try that attack for a consistent period of time.' It was an approach, which led to triumph.

The skipper had many words of praise for his erratic but talented fast bowler. 'He (Ishant) works really hard on his fitness and on his bowling and doesn't shy away from bowling long spells. Whenever you ask him to bowl, whatever situation, he gives his 100 per cent. There is no reason why he shouldn't test this line of attack. He will have to bowl a high number of overs outside India. So he will have to bowl short because he has the height. So he can exploit the bounce and put pressure on batsmen. He can add this to his armoury because it is definitely difficult to convince him.'

Everybody who heard him talk that day had the right to ask where this side of Dhoni had been hidden for so long. If he had a similarly pro-active approach overseas, wouldn't Team India have showed better results while playing in conditions that were different from the one the players had grown up in? In spite of what critics might have to say, the fact is that it 'may' have. The same approach that worked at the Lord's might have boomeranged some other day: or even at the Lord's, had some of the English batsmen not gone for self-destructive hook shots.

However, winning abroad after so many defeats was not an ordinary achievement. It showed that Dhoni's belief in his young men wasn't misplaced. They could do it. So could he, if he had them for company.

A confident young team of players who were capable of performing in overseas conditions was about to be born. Or so it seemed.

TALES OF GOD

DHONI'S STATURE OF a cricket-playing idol is the reason why Ranchi presents a peculiar problem. Too many people seem to know too much about him and few speak the truth. In the MECON stadium, which is better known than it would have been had Dhoni not played there, a couple of fairly ordinary footballers in their early 30s claim to have played with the Indian captain. While that is possible, impossible is one player's assertion that the cricketer, whose liking for milk is well known, used to drink '10-15 litres of milk every day.' Familiarity with the cricketer being the ultimate goal of many people, a footballer in his teens insists that he had played with Dhoni for the DAV Shyamali team.

If that is laughable, it is funnier to note just how many are trying to play Dhoni's inventive helicopter shot on practice pitches. Particularly distinct is one rickety kid who has been trying to hit the shot repeatedly. So what if the deliveries, after pitching one mile outside the leg stump, are way beyond his reach? He believes he can connect and send the ball flying into exosphere.

Ever since Dhoni made it to the Indian team, his changing hairstyles have been the focus of media attention. In the initial stages of his career, he used to sport long, coloured hair that cascaded to his shoulders. Later, he went for short hair, which has been his most favoured option in recent years. The Indian skipper often sports an unkempt stubble, which is visible when he steps out for the toss or chats during post match presentations. On other occasions, he is clean-shaven.

There are times when his head and beard show a mix of white and grey hair. On other occasions, the hair is jet black. Towards the latter half of 2013, he surprised everybody by getting a mohawk haircut. Within a few days, many youngsters had copied their idol without giving a serious thought to whether or not the style will be appropriate for them. Some who have acquired this style recently play football and cricket inside the stadium, turning it into a beehive of sporting activity in the evening.

Known as Mahi in the city even today, the Indian skipper may not be spending months at a stretch in his hometown, but those who know him are proud of the moments they spent with him. The stadium's ground in-charge Jena remembers each and every detail of the interaction between Mahi and his son Vijay, a promising wicketkeeper–batsman, a few years ago. 'He gave a pair of keeping gloves and a bat to my son,' he says with a smile. 'And not only that, he promised Vijay that the day he starts performing very well, he will give him an entire cricket kit.' Simple things in life make simple people happy. In spite of seeing Mahi as a child, his meeting with Vijay is an occasion that Jena will never ever forget.

The Indian captain is known to get countless fan letters from all across the country. Some of them are simply addressed to 'Mahendra Singh Dhoni, Ranchi.' These get delivered to his house. Because of Ranchi's proximity to Kolkata and also because Sourav Ganguly, popularly known as Dada, became the first player from the East Zone to lead the country with such distinction, residents are also fond of the former captain. But the difference between the two is summarised by a cab driver with amusing precision: '*Sir, Dada great thhey. Lekin Dhoni key jaisa great koi nahi hua.*' (Sir, Dada was great. But nobody has been as great as Dhoni).

Even when he was just twenty-four and the national media was describing him as the latest sensation, the local media had started speculating on the possibility of his marriage. Female fans queued up wherever he went, asking for his cell phone number. Of course, the cricketer who had no intention of marrying so early in life would oblige these girls by sharing a cell phone number: only, the number happened to be that of his brother-in-law Gautam Gupta. Gautam, who was a victim of Dhoni's pranks, would be compelled to respond with the standard phrase 'wrong number' whenever he received a hysterical telephone call from one of these girls.

Fans have their own distinct ways of paying tributes to their hero. In Dhoni's case, there was a special moment when a school student wrote a poem on him which was carried by a local newspaper. When the cricketer read it, he was touched. During those early days, Dhoni, who hadn't quite adjusted to the reality of stardom, would give autographs to anybody who asked for it. Even now, he is known to please autograph hunters to the extent he can. What he has successfully mastered is the art of eluding crowds, a quality one can only develop with experience.

Talking to *The Telegraph* during that period, his sister Jayanti, who teaches at DAV Shyamali had said, 'Dhoni never refuses request for autographs, but he is strictly against giving autographs on currency notes or palms. There have been occasions when girls have insisted that he should write on their palms, but he took out his own paper to give autographs to them,' she said.[58] With the cricketer hardly in his hometown these days, his autograph is like a rare painting which the owners treasure because chances of getting another one is remote.

In Ranchi, the Indian captain makes news for the strangest of reasons. A couple of years after he had started playing for the national team, he had gone for a haircut to Kaya Beauty Parlour, an upmarket beauty salon located in Hari Om Towers, a shopping complex in the city's Circular Road that had been inaugurated by the former chief minister Babulal Marandi the year before. He reached the salon at 11.45 am. Within minutes of his arrival, the news spread. The complex also houses many coaching institutes. Youngsters studying there assembled outside the salon for a glimpse of their icon. That the Ranchi Women's College is situated opposite the complex enhanced the problem manifold with many girls joining the crowd.

Controlling the fans took a lot more time than one would have imagined. As minutes passed, the number of people continued to increase. Dhoni had no choice but to remain locked up inside. The salon had to pull down its shutters and stop doing business for hours. The management called the police, which finally helped him find a way out of the premises at 5.15 pm.

Before he became a client of Kaya, Dhoni used to visit a far more affordable salon. The name is a seriously funny one:

[58]'Wrong number for star suitors—Proposals pouring in but pin-up bachelor boy not ready', *The Telegraph*, 4 November 2005. http://www. telegraphindia.com/1051104/asp/ranchi/story_5435092.asp (accessed 22 December 2014).

Manly Beauty Parlour. *The Telegraph* spoke to an employee of the salon who rued the loss of its most valued customer. '*Woh toh ab bade aadmi ho gaye hain* (He has become famous now),' said Guddu, a staff at Manly Beauty Parlour, which used to be Dhoni's favourite haunt before attaining celebrity status. A small parlour's loss was a bigger one's gain.[59]

Ranchi deifies Dhoni, which the yoga guru Baba Ramdev realized while visiting the city to conduct a camp for his numerous followers. The Jharkhand Government had gifted a plot of land to Dhoni as a reward for his cricketing excellence. The cricketer had come down to receive the allotment letter from the then state Chief Minister Arjun Munda and Baba Ramdev, before the fifth yoga session consisting of laughter exercises and 'singhasan' began.

The moment Dhoni reached the dais, the atmosphere changed. The practitioners, who had been following the baba's instructions carefully earlier, tried to find a way to come close to the cricketer. The baba asked them to complete their exercises first. But with Dhoni around, nobody cared. Touching him became the bigger priority. Few cared about the last session any longer.

Realising that he had lost complete control over the crowd, Ramdev made a diplomatic move. Instead of insisting on guiding his followers, he started praising Dhoni. He called Dhoni a 'saput' (good son) of the nation and requested him to sit next to him so that everybody could have a close look at

---

[59]'Much ado about Dhoni's hair—wicket-keeper chooses an up-market salon for his long locks', The Telegraph, Arti Sahuliyar, 10 November 2006. http://www.telegraphindia.com/1061110/asp/ranchi/story_6980707.asp (accessed 22 December 2014).

their favourite star. He started mouthing inanities like '*Dhoni ke balley ne bahuton ko dhhoya hai*' (Dhoni's bat has thrashed many bowlers). He told the crowd that just like the Pakistan President Pervez Musharraf had become a fan of Dhoni's hair, even he was a fan of the cricketer's hair. The reason why even he kept his hair long!

Ramdev didn't stop there. He asked Dhoni to practise exercises like 'kapal bhati' and 'anulom vilom' to increase his concentration. He also blessed his parents, and added that his evening camp had been organised so that Jharkhand could give more Dhonis to India in future. Disturbed by the sight of the cricketer were those who viewed his presence during a yoga camp as an unnecessary intrusion. But they were hugely outnumbered by others who felt blessed because of his attendance, having forgotten that there was another session left—which was abandoned anyway.

Since his teenage days, Dhoni had been enamoured by two-wheelers. As a school-going boy, he used to drive his father's scooter. After he started receiving a stipend from the CCL, he managed to save enough money to be able to buy a second-hand bike. It was only after he became a part of the Indian team that he started indulging in his passion for collecting and driving any bike of his choice. If one were to trust self-indulgent myth-weavers in Ranchi, the cricketer owns anything between five hundred and one thousand bikes, the number depending on how big a liar one is talking to.

A 650-cc Yamaha Thunderbird and a Bullet Machismo were among his initial purchases. But the bike which attracted the maximum media attention was the Confederate X132 Hellcat, a muscle bike which is also owned by Hollywood superstar Brad Pitt and former England footballer David

Beckham. Among those in his collection of rebuilt and customised bikes, Dhoni is known to be fond of a Harley Davidson. A car freak as well, his soft corner for his Hummer has been discussed in the media. Not just cars and bikes, every luxury is at his doorstep. Once upon a time, he was just another young lad from Ranchi's Shyamali colony, but now Dhoni is living his dream.

Spending a little time among Ranchi's residents can easily reveal just how many stories about the man's life is stored inside his fans' minds. A hotel waiter comments on the 'unfair' treatment of the establishment that had imposed a fine of Rs 90 on him for driving a Mitsubishi Pajero SUV with tinted glasses. Prior to that, he had also been fined for his Scorpio which too had tinted glasses. During the earlier occasion, his elder brother Narendra had tried to convince the police that Dhoni needed to use such glasses as a precautionary measure since wherever he went, he was regularly mobbed. But the reasoning failed to work. In fact, the Pajero and the Scorpio often travelled simultaneously so that people on the streets couldn't figure out which one to follow and which not to.

While the story of a fine of Rs 90 for flouting vehicle-related rules continues to circulate in Ranchi, what is conveniently ignored, for reasons best known to the locals, is what happened thereafter. The fine was waived later, with the Senior Superintendent of Police NP Singh clarifying that the cricketer had been permitted to retain the screen on his vehicle for two days, while he was in the city, because of security reasons.

From Dhoni's fine to his inability to complete his college degree: each and every episode in the cricketer's life is common knowledge. After he had become the captain of the Indian team in all formats of the game, the cricketer, who still hasn't completed his graduation degree from Gossner College, got himself enrolled for the Office Management and Secretarial Practices course from St Xavier's College, Ranchi. Although it is a three-year course, the management gave Dhoni a maximum of five years to complete it.

The supportive college administration went all out to assist the Indian captain. It exempted the cricketer from attending classes and even allowed him to take the tests according to his convenience. Study material was provided to him. He was allowed to prepare for the exams and inform the college whenever he was ready to appear for the examinations so that the question papers could be set accordingly. That St Xavier's College, which is well known for its academic environment both within Jharkhand and outside, took such a drastic measure to help the cricketer is unthinkable. Inspite of that, however, Dhoni failed to find time for the course. That he wants to complete his college education is known to everybody. However, had he completed the course, who would have been able to hire him as his Personal Assistant anyway? That is a common joke in Ranchi among those who know him that the cricketer had taken admission in order to get an actual and not an honorary degree.

The Jharkhand government has showered the Indian captain with honours. After the Indian team won the ICC World Cup under his leadership in 2011, the government not only rewarded him with an honorary doctorate but also gave him the Jharkhand Khel Ratna award along with a gift of land. The cricketer was authorised to choose his plot of land in any part of Jharkhand that suited him. The announcement epitomises the royal treatment that Dhoni has received in his state both from the masses and the government alike.

Reading up the coverage of the local media on each and every sportsperson is humanly impossible. However, it is possible to argue that hardly any sportsperson barring Tendulkar in Mumbai and Ganguly in Kolkata has received the kind of local media attention that Dhoni has. So detailed is the reporting that should you talk to any of his devotees, don't be surprised if you are told that the cricketer's family had promised to gift a Mitsubishi Pajero to a local priest if India won the World Cup. Or, something equally interesting which shows that each newspaper seems to have a reporter who concentrates on getting Dhoni stories for the insatiably hungry readers.

When Hiren Patel, the winner of the 'FritoLay (Uncle Chipps and Kurkure) Chala Change Ka Chakkar' competition was about to come down to Ranchi in 2008, the media latched on to the story. Considering the number of Dhoni stories that bombard the local newspapers, talking about Patel, who had won the right to 'exchange his life' with the cricketer for a day, was inevitable. *The Pioneer* reported, 'Mahi who is the brand ambassador of FritoLay India that has five flagship brands--Lay's, Kurkure, Cheetos, Uncle Chipps and Lehar's--will exchange life with Patel by spending a day at his Mumbai's Malad East residence on March 15.' The report went into each and every detail, like mentioning that Patel will get an opportunity to move around in Dhoni's Harley Davidson motorbike and SUVs such as Mitshubishi Pajero and Mahindra Scorpio.

It expressed concern over whether or not the 'Ranchi Rambo's dogs would allow him to come near them' and also informed, 'Soon after arriving at Ranchi airport, Patel will be taken to... various other places where Dhoni frequents like MECON stadium, DAV Shyamali School, Kaya parlour,

Chashme Shahi restaurant and Madhuban dhaba on Ranchi Patna highway.'[60] Such stories make the Dhoni-loving Ranchi resident a walking-talking encyclopaedia on the man. If imagination plays a supplementary role, a local can boast that he has been to Dhoni's place or sat and chatted with him in Madhuban Dhaba several times. Hence, he is luckier than Patel. But then, exaggeration and lying can be experienced anywhere in the world. The only difference is that in Ranchi, too many of them have Dhoni as the subject.

The Dhonis have changed quite a few houses over the years. Still, every place where he once lived has a distinguishing identity card: the house number which separates it from the rest of the pack since that is where the cricketer once lived. Years after the family moved out of the small two-room house numbered N-171 in Shyamali colony, it still has the occasional visitor who turns up just to see the house from outside.

For a long time, the consultancy giant MECON took pride in saying 'M for Mahi, M for MECON.' Even after his father Paan Singh had retired, MECON tried its best to ensure that the star continued to stay in Shyamali colony which is strictly meant for active company employees. After Dhoni had started playing for India in the ODIs, the Dhoni family decided to shift to a three-bedroom accommodation in Kilburn Colony on a monthly rent of Rs 5,600.

Not at all willing to give up, MECON moved in. The Dhonis were given a spacious bungalow E-25 in the same locality. If N-171 was a tiny house, E-25 was an independent bungalow with a garage in which the star could park his

---

[60]'Ranchi to have a new Mahi for a day', *The Pioneer* (Ranchi edition), 6 March 2008.

vehicles. Today, E-25 is the second destination of Dhoni's admirers who, in their quest for knowing as much as they possibly can, go to see the bungalow so that they can describe how it looks to other Dhoni fans who possibly do not stay in Ranchi.

For cricket lovers, Ranchi's most important centre of pilgrimage is the Indian captain's mansion in Harmu Housing Colony. In a city filled with fanatical admirers, Dhoni has no other choice but to seek intense privacy and avoid being seen by the curious passers-by. The house reportedly has seven or eight bedrooms, a swimming pool, a nice garden and a gymnasium, the last being an absolute must since the cricketer cannot go for workouts to a public gym.

A major part of the land on which the house has been built was the state government's gift to Dhoni, which is not a pleasant thought for everybody. A nattily dressed man walking slowly by the house cribs, '*Sarkar ka bus chaley toh isko poora Ranchi dey dey.*' (If the government has its way, it would gift the entire city to the cricketer).

Good performers in major cricketing centres have received similar gifts of land from the government. But for Ranchi, such a reward for a cricketer is a novelty. However, numerous Dhoni admirers, who know the exact size of the house and the story about the gift of land, are anything but critical. They worship Dhoni. They see him as the man who has conquered the final frontier in cricket.

For them, he is God.

LEADER OF MEN

MORE THAN THREE years after its last overseas victory, India under MS Dhoni ended its winless streak abroad by defeating Alastair Cook's English side by 95 runs in the second Test at the Lord's on 21 July 2014. But, India's win didn't erase the question mark to his approach to captaincy in Test matches overseas.

Having said that, what is undeniable is that he is a master strategist in the shorter versions, has won several Tests in spite of his poor overseas record, and has acquired the reputation for being the best finisher in the shorter version of the game the world has ever seen. Taking over when most of the batting greats of yesteryears had started losing their historically proven touch, he had to create a team with newcomers. That he has, although how many of them will eventually make a significant impact like their predecessors did, remains to be seen. Who are these players?

Among them is Ravindra Jadeja whose inconsistency is a worry. Whether or not he should be used as a bowler who can pick up wickets in Tests abroad is an issue that needs to be debated. What can be said for sure is that Jadeja needs to add variety to his bowling so that it is possible to set attacking fields for him which will present some difficulties to batsmen in spin-unfriendly conditions. Besides, Jadeja also needs to justify the team's expectations from his batting ability which has enabled him to score three triple hundreds in domestic cricket. That he has played few knocks of substance in the international arena is an area which needs improvement.

Slowly but steadily, Bhuvaneshwar Kumar is turning out to be a huge asset for the team. Visually unthreatening, Kumar, who bowls at a pace which is fractionally faster than slow medium bowling, has a huge gift which can catch the best of batsmen off-guard. He can swing the ball both ways, and chooses his options very intelligently. As a batsman coming in at number nine, he surprised everybody in the India–England series by scoring three half-centuries in the first two Tests.

Too much has been made of Kumar's important century in a domestic match. But when a relatively inexperienced player, whose number defines him as a bonafide tailender, can take on the likes of fast bowlers such as Stuart Broad and James Anderson and score 50s in unfamiliar conditions, it will be only fair to admit that his batting can add a lot of value to the team. If morning shows the day, his temperament is such that he won't fade away from the international scene anytime soon.

To describe Rohit Sharma is very difficult. On the one hand, he is phenomenally talented, a young man who has every stroke in the textbook to offer and more. On the other, the quality of his batting fluctuates from one extreme to the other. There are days when he is simply sublime—so audacious and attractive in his strokeplay that best of fielders stand and watch as the ball penetrates each and every corner of the ground. Then, there are those days when Sharma cannot put up with the easiest of deliveries. Besides, whenever he walks out to bat and even if he is batting at his best, nobody knows when he will hit that one rash stroke, lose his wicket and return to the pavilion. He has what it takes to become a long-distance runner on the track of international cricket. But, the big question is, does he want to become one? If so, he has to learn to put a price on his wicket.

Why Cheteshwar Pujara has been branded as a Test specialist is a mystery. In the ODIs, if not the Twenty20s, it can be argued that he can be fielded as a batsman who plays the sheet anchor's role while getting his runs at a reasonably fast clip. For that to happen, however, Pujara must get opportunities to play without a break in the format so that he can gain confidence and settle in that role. In Test matches, however, he has shown an appetite for playing big knocks which is an important requirement for the present Indian team. Most importantly, Pujara can bat for longer periods than anybody else. While calling him the Dravid of the future is taking things a little too far too soon, Pujara is most certainly somebody who has the talent, sincerity and application to score runs and hold one end up while others play around him. How many times he will manage to do it is a question only time can answer.

About Shikhar Dhawan, let there be no doubt that he is a talented batsman. The problem with Dhawan is that while his technical loopholes are becoming increasingly visible, he also gets out to that odd loose shot a little too often. After his brilliant show at the outset of his career, he has not been able sustain the momentum.

Ravichandran Ashwin is a dilemma. In home conditions, he has proved to be a matchwinner. But he still needs to mature to make an impact in overseas conditions where assistance to the spinner is nominal or even virtually non-existent. He has shown that he is a more-than-useful bat at number eight. As he works on his bowling, Ashwin also needs to apply himself and do some serious practice to qualify as a decent-enough fielder. At the moment, he is bad in just about any position.

Murali Vijay, at his best, is about style and elegance. Even when he is subdued because of particularly hostile bowling of the kind where he must negotiate since he is an opener, he has come across as a solid batsman on quite a few occasions. His defence is good, but that doesn't prevent him from capitalising on bad balls with his vast range of strokes. The problem with Vijay is that he has experienced quite a few failures. In no way does that disprove the fact that he is a seriously gifted player whose contribution can be vital for the Indian team.

Far away from the limelight is the quiet and resourceful Ajinkya Rahane. Part of the team in transition, Rahane is practically invisible until he takes a fine catch, but more importantly, gets those important runs for his squad. It can be said that this immensely gifted batsman has failed to deliver on more occasions than he has passed. But, watching him bat is a clear indication that he will definitely go a long way. His USP is his pleasingly calm mindset, a quality not many young players share.

Among Dhoni's fast bowlers, Mohammed Shami has what few Indian bowlers have: raw pace. His problem is his proclivity for bowling that one bad delivery in almost every over, his personal favourite being a full-length one which drifts down the leg side and allows the batsman to get some free runs. Shami's talent is visible to one and all, but he needs to make sure that his line and length don't waver on crucial occasions.

Way back in the 2007-08 season against Australia, Ishant Sharma had tormented Ricky Ponting with a memorable spell in Perth. Facing his in-swinging deliveries, that darted into

Ponting, was a struggle for the latter, who eventually got out, caught by Dravid at second slip. It was a spell of bowling that few cricket lovers can forget, although what happened thereafter gradually turned into a reason for worry and distress for the Indian cricketing establishment.

In the second Test at the Lord's against England in 2014, it was Ishant, with his spell of 7/74, who was persuaded by Dhoni to bowl short-pitched stuff in an effort to demolish the hosts. The skipper supported him with an attacking field, and England succumbed. But Ishant continues to be a riddle for everybody, his mind-boggling inconsistency being an area of concern nobody has been able to successfully address so far.

Raina is younger and a proven star in the shorter versions; as a matter of fact, he is among the best we have. What he must do is shape up as a Test batsman whenever he gets an opportunity, lest he is compelled to end his career as a shorter-version specialist in the future. He is far more adept at handling the short ball than he used to be, which is a good-enough reason to allow him to make a comeback in the five-day format should the opportunity arise.

While those waiting at the fringes include names such as batting all-rounder Stuart Binny and fast bowler Varun Aaron, who might have grown into a serious threat for the established quickies, those discussed above are the main players in the Test team, which lacks batsmen of the class of Tendulkar, Dravid, Ganguly, Sehwag and Laxman with the exception of Kohli and possibly Pujara in future and spinners such as Kumble and Harbhajan, whose effectiveness and skills aren't unknown to anybody. Among those who are still playing, it will take more than a miracle to revive Sehwag's career in the international circuit, while Harbhajan has also left his best days behind.

Yuvraj has played a major part in the shorter version, winning matches for India in both ODIs and Twenty20s with the sort of performances that can make anybody proud. But he is gradually fading away from the scene, though the chances of making a comeback.

As a leader, Dhoni had to deal with his seniors' decline in form for a long period in his career. With an eye on creating a team for the future, he had to take some seriously tough decisions about dropping seniors. The team, as we see it today, is a young one.

Off the field, Dhoni has been typically down to earth while assessing his own contribution as the captain. In an interview to Wisden India, he spoke about how he perceives his role, 'Of course, I take it as a job responsibility, I have been given the responsibility and I try to fulfil it to the best potential that I have got. As an individual, you will make mistakes and as a captain, I feel it is very important that if you commit a mistake, you go out there and admit it. It won't always go your way. The captain decides on something but it is somebody else who has to fulfil the job. Ultimately, it depends on the person and how he responds to the situation. You try to be honest to yourself, you read the game and decide something. If it doesn't work, you stand up and take the responsibility because that's what your job needs you to do.'[61] Ever since he started playing for India, his assessment of situations has been precise and analytical. This one was no different.

Not many times in his entire career has Captain Cool

[61]'Dhoni shuts out off-field issues', *Wisden India*, Abhishek Purohit, 5 April 2014. http://www.espncricinfo.com/world-t20/content/story/735045.html (accessed 22 December 2014).

lost his cool. While those who have seen him in his younger days agree that he was a level-headed boy who was desperate to win and never got perturbed, Dhoni said the opposite of the public perception about him. With the passage of time, he has 'learned how to control his emotion,' he said. He added, '(Gradually) I found dealing with emotions easier. I feel it is important because in a game, there are so many stages where you don't want to take a decision emotionally. Practically, you decide what's the best option.'

Dhoni has been able to create a unit out of a young Indian team which believes in him, and has been a hugely successful leader as well. Vineet Nayar, Founder CEO, HCL Technologies and Founder, SAMPARK Foundation, explains his performance in the context of leadership in a broader sense, 'Leadership has three levels/types with inspirational leadership being at the top of the heap. The first is efficiency which, in the context of cricket, implies that a leader must strive to be the best batsman, best bowler or the best all-rounder in his team. Then comes effectiveness. An effective leader is someone who puts a team of efficient people together and makes it perform at 150, not 100 per cent of its true potential.'

Nayar adds, 'The final tier is that of the inspirational leader. Inspirational leaders are rare, and they ensure that the team performs at 500 per cent of its true potential. While Sunil Gavaskar and Kapil Dev were effective leaders, Sourav Ganguly and Mahendra Singh Dhoni have gone beyond effectiveness.'

Harsh Goenka, Chairman, RPG Enterprises, speaks along similar lines while comparing the role of a corporate leader with that of a person leading a unit in a team sport such as cricket, 'Leadership is the ability to convince the team to own your vision. This holds true in business and also in sport because the commonality is that there is constant interaction between people with varied ideas, opinions, approach and beliefs.'

He adds, 'The starting point is to have team members with skills who complement one another. A leader must have the knack of identifying the talent in each person and utilizing it to ensure that the whole is greater than the sum of parts.' By identifying players and assigning roles to them, there is very little doubt that Dhoni has created a structure which can be expected to deliver better results in the long run: which will hopefully include better performances in the longer version in overseas conditions which has been a dark spot in his otherwise glittering career.

Explaining Dhoni's success as a team leader, Goenka recalls that famous example which has turned into an enjoyable part of cricketing folklore today. He says, 'He has foresight. He leads from the front. He has taken risks. He stands by his men. For instance, he promoted himself in batting order in front of an in-form Yuvraj Singh in the World Cup final against Sri Lanka in 2011. The decision surprised many, especially the match being a World Cup final, but Dhoni had played and practiced with Muttiah Muralitharan in his IPL franchise and knew he would come to bowl soon. Knowing Yuvraj's weakness against top class spin and his own knowledge of Murali, Dhoni came in and anchored the team home safe with a World Cup in hand.'

One major question comes up for analyses during discussions very often. Who is a better skipper: Ganguly or Dhoni? The reason is clear. While Ganguly built a strong team after the match-fixing crisis, Dhoni is seen as the true inheritor of the the former's legacy. When analysed in terms of performance as the skipper in both Tests and ODIs, these two come across as competitors. Harsha Bhogle agrees that this question is very difficult to answer.

Bhogle says, 'That is a tough call because you don't know how Dhoni would have been in that situation. Ganguly handled it well, but if Dhoni had the sort of players that Ganguly did, he might have too. This is not to belittle Ganguly's role which was crucial. Ganguly's great strength lay in nurturing people like Zaheer, Sehwag, Harbhajan and Yuvraj.' But he adds, 'I think you will find that players like Ashwin and Raina and Kohli might say the same things about Dhoni. I think his great skill as captain has been to make younger people feel secure and make people's roles clear.'

While saying that India have been very lucky to have captains such as Ganguly through Dravid and Kumble to Dhoni in recent times, Bhogle gives an interesting example which echoes Goenka's emphasis on assigning roles to players, 'I remember Dwayne Bravo telling me that he felt very comfortable even playing a relatively smaller role at Chennai Super Kings (this was a couple of years ago) because he knew exactly what was expected of him.'

Former Indian hockey captain, whose stickwork mesmerised the opposition during his peak as a player, Dhanraj Pillay, believes that Ganguly has an edge over Dhoni as a leader. Remembering his own days as a hockey skipper, Pillay says, 'As a captain, I was aggressive. So I feel that if Dhoni as a skipper is disappointed with a player's bowling or fielding, he must give some indication of how he feels. Personally, I think that while both Ganguly and Dhoni have shown excellent captaincy skills, the former during his days had introduced a combative spirit which is very important. That, according to me, makes him a better captain because Dhoni must incorporate that approach in his style.'

Too much criticism about Dhoni's poor overseas record irks former Indian player and former Chairman of the Selection Committee of the BCCI Chandu Borde, who firmly believes that 'Dhoni is the kind of lad who has his own ideas about how to lead his team in any particular situation. He does not believe in textbook-guided leadership, relies on his instincts, and performs brilliantly.'

Talking about his performance overseas, he says, 'When the Indian players go abroad, the conditions are different. The team gets very little time to acclimatise to the bouncy pitches, for instance. Likewise, when visitors come to India, they have to deal with very tough situations. Losing matches in unfamiliar conditions is natural, and we must not single out Dhoni for it. On his part, he does an excellent job.'

Yesteryear Indian wicketkeeper and former Chairman of the Selection Committee of the BCCI Kiran More also insists that there is no reason to be critical about the man. 'As a captain, he has done astoundingly well in the subcontinent because the Indian batting does very well in such conditions. Likewise, his spinners also play a very important role in winning Test matches. But abroad, he has gone on the defensive at times even when the match seems to be tilted in India's favour. This has happened not because he is incapable of taking decisions but since the team has major shortcomings in the resources department.'

Statistical evidence shows that India's performance in away matches—Tests in particular—has nothing to write home about. However, More believes that gunning for the leader is highly unfair, 'Dhoni has a terrific cricketing brain. His planning and decisions are very well thought out. I wish he had far better support than he actually does,' he says. The big problem, according to More, is India's bowling. 'India's bowling doesn't have those two key elements that can win matches abroad: variety and surprise. Jadeja and Ashwin continue to play as spinners, but they haven't achieved much success outside the subcontinent. Meanwhile, Amit Mishra is a permanent traveller, who is seldom seen in the playing eleven outside the country. Some serious thinking, therefore, needs to be done on that front instead of criticising the manner in which he leads the team on the field.'

Among the cricketers from the past, who have been observing Dhoni's emergence since the days when he had started out, is former India batsman Abbas Ali Baig, who initially saw him as a 'bit of a wild youth who could hit sixes at will.' Since then, years have gone by. The young man of yesteryears who has been leading the Indian team for quite sometime has experienced all sorts of highs and lows a cricketer possibly can. 'A peace-loving guy with an undemonstrative demeanour, one thing that is a little amiss is the manner in which he lets things drag in Test matches which is not the case with his leadership in the shorter versions of the game,' says Baig.

Bhogle, who has been witnessing his growth as a skipper for years, appears to agree with Baig's assessment of Dhoni's leadership in the longer version, 'It is tough to say that while watching from so far away. But he does give the impression that he doesn't trust his bowlers entirely and so the defensive Plan B is always round the corner.'

However, Baig believes that Dhoni must continue until a younger player is ready to take over. As he adds, 'There is no doubt that he does take a lot of responsibility on his shoulders. For the next couple of years, I see him as someone who will lead the team. Among the younger lot, Virat Kohi is being projected as the frontrunner.'

While some see Dhoni's calmness as absence of enterprise in leadership, others believe that it is an extraordinary quality which sets him apart and helps the team. Borde offers an interesting reason, 'Bowlers in particular don't like it when their skipper gets upset because they have been having a bad day. If you keep that in mind, Dhoni's calmness is a great quality. He knows that he is a sportsperson and that any team will experience successes and failures. So he carries on with the game, which is beneficial for everybody.'

Goenka says, 'Everybody has faced adversity at some time or the other. Few can have complete control over their nerves. When the mind is calm, one can think better. Dhoni has demonstrated time and again that he is in control of his emotions and this phenomenal ability has come to his advantage many times.'

Nayar believes that the Indian skipper's calmness has 'a purpose.' He reasons, 'Dhoni's calmness is a strategy. He knows he is leading an inspired team. As is the case with the captain of a river rafting team who communicates with his team without talking—understandably so, since his voice cannot rise above the sound of the current—Dhoni communicates without showing his feelings and talking to individual players who already know what their captain is thinking and what he wants from them.'

The focus on Dhoni's failures in away Test matches has been such that all his good qualities, which have engineered so many spectacular triumphs, tend to get swept under the carpet. More emphasises on Dhoni as a performer, a quality which has allowed him to have such a united young team at his disposal.

He says, 'As a keeper, he has been very effective. If someone criticises his keeping after 500 dismissals in international cricket, it cannot be highlighted as his weakness.'

Dhoni may not be a Pujara or a Vijay, who are supposed to anchor the innings in the best way possible. But he has been able to execute his well-defined responsibility as a batsman very well quite often. 'When under pressure as a batsman in the shorter version, he is the best in the world. In Tests, he is the most important batsman in the lower middle order who has played many significant knocks for his country. Such performances have shown he leads his side from the front,' says More.

Nayar reasons that Dhoni's performance as an individual has played a major role in making him an inspirational leader. He uses Ganguly's example to establish his argument, 'Following the match-fixing scandal that had rocked the cricketing establishment, Ganguly built the momentum of the Indian team and gave it confidence. After he took over as the captain, he was an inspirational leader for quite sometime. But he lost out once his core competence—that of a batsman—deteriorated. Had that not happened, he would have continued to be a fantastic leader.'

He extends this argument to explain why Dhoni has been able to motivate his team. 'An inspirational leader has to be efficient in order to retain his influence. Dhoni, for instance, is the best finisher of the game in the shorter one-day version. The day he loses his touch or becomes a bad keeper and a failure as a batsman in Test matches, he will stop being inspirational,' he affirms.

Whether or not Dhoni must continue to lead Team India in Tests continued to be a hotly-debated subject in the cricketing circles. During the New Zealand tour of 2014, Dravid told ESPNcricinfo.com that Dhoni must realize that he has to 'risk it all' if he 'wants to win Test matches abroad,' while former New Zealand star Martin Crowe analysed, '...I would say that if India want to defend the next World Cup, I think MS Dhoni needs a rest somewhere, at some point, not necessarily from playing, but maybe it could be by not captaining the Test side for a period leading into the World Cup, to refresh him so that he can hit the ground running for that World Cup. So there's a couple of things to ponder there.'

Crowe added, 'I think he's an absolutely gifted player, a marvel at times, given all the formats that he plays, but I do wonder sometimes about how he regards Test cricket. Just a point that I'd like to throw in there. Overall, MS Dhoni is an incredible cricketer, and I think that the main fact is that he probably can't keep doing every format from here on in.'[62] Crowe's comment showed that he didn't endorse the idea of Dhoni leading the Test side, and in fact, had doubts about whether or not Dhoni views the longer version seriously enough.

The Indian captain's job is such that he is destined to be under the spotlight. But, truth be told, Dhoni has been able to build a unit of players who can take the Indian team in the right direction in future. Goenka says, 'During the transition phase, Dhoni has formed a formidable core group with captain-in-waiting Virat Kohli, Suresh Raina, Ravindra Jadeja, Cheteshwar Pujara, R Ashwin, Shikhar Dhawan and of late Rohit Sharma. He hasn't chopped and changed his side

<hr>

[62]'Dravid: Dhoni needs to take risks to win overseas', *ESPNcricinfo.com*, 8 February 2014. http://www.espncricinfo.com/new-zealand-v-india-2014/content/story/720369.html (accessed 23 December 2014).

even after terrible losses against England and Australia. He rallied by the talent he believed in, and didn't mind making tough choices of dropping pros like Harbhajan Singh, Virender Sehwag and Gautam Gambhir.'

Being a very private person, chances were no one would know about his cricketing plans until he suddenly made an announcement. On 30 December 2014, Dhoni announced his retirement from Test cricket with immediate effect. His decision was conveyed by a BCCI press release which read: 'One of India's greatest Test captains under whose leadership India became the No. 1 team in the test rankings, MS Dhoni, has decided to retire from Test cricket citing the strain of playing all formats of cricket.' It added, 'BCCI, while respecting the decision of MS Dhoni to retire from Test cricket, wishes to thank him for his enormous contribution to Test cricket and the laurels that he has brought to India. Virat Kohli will be the captain of the Indian team for the fourth and final Test against Australia to be played in Sydney.'

BCCI Secretary Sanjay Patel told PTI that the Indian captain was a 'bit emotional while announcing his decision in the dressing room.' But he added that Dhoni would continue to lead the team in the shorter format. The new Test captain Virat Kohli is now in the hot seat. The management and selectors see him as a player who will eventually take over as the leader of Team India in all three formats of the game once Dhoni calls it a day like every cricketer inevitably must.

Before he left the Test arena for good, Dhoni gave a peep into his mindset which his fans will never forget. In the last innings of his last Test match, he had fought hard with Ashwin and remained unbeaten on 24 to guide the team to a draw. Before he went out to bat, he would have known that he would announce his retirement from Test matches. But he remained as calm as ever, and prevented India from going 0-3 down in the series before making way for young Kohli. Dhoni's approach to his last Test innings defines the legacy he will leave behind when he eventually retires from all the versions of the game. By making a statement of his temperament, approach and sense of responsibility, he once again showed what a leader must do when he swims against the tide.

Soon after his decision became public, tweets from former cricketers flooded the social media. Tendulkar tweeted, 'well done on a wonderful career in test cricket @msdhoni. Always enjoyed playing together. Next target 2015 WC my friend!!' Kumble, his predecessor, remarked, 'Chennai 2 G, Great career MSD @msdhoni retired as captain. Way 2 go! Well done buddy on a fantastic test inning! Good luck!' Mathew Hayden said, '@msdhoni Test Cricket will miss your unique persona, your calm presence blended with your playful spirit and exceptional skill.'

Speaking to ESPNcricinfo.com, Dravid said, 'He was a captain I enjoyed playing under.' He added, 'One of the things I liked about MS was, what you saw was what you got. Very uncomplicated, always led by example. One of the things I really liked about playing under MS was that he never asked you to do anything that he himself didn't do.' Echoing Bhogle's sentiments, he added, 'And he's been an inspiration. If there are kids in small towns today dreaming and aspiring for great things, not only in cricket but in various fields, then MS Dhoni has a lot to do with it.' [63]

---

[63]'"Dhoni led by example, not rhetoric"—Dravid', *ESPNcricinfo.com*, 30 December 2014. http://www.espncricinfo.com/india/content/story/815145.htm (accessed on 31 December 2014)

The timing of Dhoni's announcement must have shocked people, but right now, his focus is on Team India's next big goal: a special performance in the ICC World Cup 2015. He would like to go out there, guide his troops, and try his best to pull off a magic trick or two from his bag whenever the team needs one.

THE STAR AND HIS FUTURE

IN THE HISTORY of Indian cricket, MS Dhoni is a unique phenomenon. To say that he comes from a lower-middle-class background is putting it mildly. He grew up playing cricket in Ranchi, which hadn't produced a single cricketer who was good enough to play for India before Dhoni came along. At the domestic first-class level, he played most of his cricket for Bihar, a highly mediocre team. In order to support his family, he even worked as a ticket collector, and did platform duty at the Kharagpur Railway station. The first important team he ever led was that of India in the inaugural World Twenty20.

During his days as a promising cricketer in his hometown, he could not afford to buy a decent cricket kit. But such has been his growth and popularity that he is the highest paid athlete in India by a long distance. In fact, he was ranked 22 among the Top 100 highest paid athletes in the world by Forbes, whose calculations included money earned from salaries and winnings and endorsements between June 2013 and June 2014.

Dhoni's total earnings including endorsements worth $ 26 million touched $ 30 million, the kind of money a cricketer can only hope to earn in his dreams in spite of the advent of the IPL. Forbes highlighted '...his deals with leading brands like Spartan Sports and Amity University in late 2013 reportedly worth a combined USD four million annually, up from the USD one million Reebok was paying previously.'

In April 2014, *The Hindustan Times* reported that the Indian skipper's brand value had 'jumped by almost 60%' in the last four months and that his endorsement fees had touched a new high of Rs 13 crore from 'about Rs 8 crore per deal per annum.' Speaking to the newspaper, Arun Pandey, his close friend and chairman, Rhiti Sports Management, said, 'Dhoni has recently signed deals with six to eight brands where he will get a share of revenues generated by those brands.'[64] If one sees such figures in the context of the fact that Dhoni's endorsement fee is the second highest after the Indian megastar Aamir Khan, who charges Rs 15 crore per deal, it is easy to understand why he is way ahead of his counterparts in terms of his popularity and impact as a cricketer.

The face of several major brands today, Dhoni had started his career by signing deals with GE Money, Cherry Blossom, Reebok, Pepsi and TVS among others. In an effective and touching Cherry Blossom ad, he had showed up in a Railway uniform and talked about how he could have easily continued to be in a profession he had left behind.

By the time it was 2010, Dhoni had overtaken Tendulkar to create a new record. A *Business Today* report which talks about Pandey's role in building Brand Dhoni states, 'Dhoni signed on with Rhiti for a minimum guarantee of Rs 210 crore over three years. Officially, Dhoni had now overtaken

---

[64]'Brand Dhoni overtakes Virat Kohli', *The Hindustan Times*, Himani Chandna Gurtoo, 11 April 2014. http://www.hindustantimes.com/sports-news/cricketnews/brand-dhoni-overtakes-virat-kohli/article1-1206787.aspx (accessed 23 December 2014).

Tendulkar, who held the previous record of Rs 180 crore over three years under a deal with Iconix in 2006.'[65] He is what millions across the country want to be. The advertisers have been cashing in on this USP, making him richer by the day.

A keen follower of sports, the Indian skipper has invested in many sports-related ventures. His latest acquisition is Ranchi Rays, a new Hockey India League franchise, for which he has partnered with the Sahara India Pariwar. He also co-owns Chennaiyin FC, an Indian Super League football franchise. Then, there is Mahi Racing Team India, which takes part in superbike racing, the Supersport FIM World Championship. These are business investments no doubt; yet, Dhoni must be credited for playing an active part in promoting sports other than cricket already.

If Dhoni continues to be the focus of attention because of his cricket or even his bikes, marriage and investments, it is because of the game which has gifted him with enormous success and adulation. Such is his popularity that a film on him titled *M.S. Dhoni: The Untold Story* starring Sushant Singh Rajput will be releasing in 2015. At 33, however, the Indian skipper decided to reduce the burden on him by relinquishing Test captaincy. Having led his side to triumphs in all the formats of the game, which includes ones in ICC tournaments, he has already set a steep target which will be exceptionally difficult to emulate.

Being in the limelight has had its share of disadvantages,

---

[65]'Mahendra Singh Dhoni: The god of big deals', *Business Today*, Suveen K Sinha, Edition dated 14 April 2013. http://businesstoday.intoday.in/story/celebrity-marketing-cricketer-ms-dhoni-endorsing-brands/1/193100.html (accessed 23 December 2014).

and Dhoni knows its implications as well as anyone does and can. In his hometown, which he dearly loves, he cannot move around as freely as he would have loved to. Vandalism after India loses an important match isn't new to his family any longer. Such has been his schedule that he seldom manages to spend time at home, a fact of life he has learned to accept. For him, the only bright side is that he won't be playing the game forever.

From being a boy from an ordinary family to becoming one of the richest sportspersons in the world, Dhoni's journey has been a long, eventful and struggle-filled one which has turned him into the heart-throb of Larger India. Today, what he doesn't lack is money. But what he doesn't have at his disposal is time. Being a decent-enough student, who had secured a first division in his Class X exams and nearly got a first division in Class XII in 1999, he had applied to Gossner College in Ranchi to pursue his Bachelors in Commerce degree for the 1999-2002 batch. Until today, he hasn't been able to fulfill his dream.

As Dhoni gets ready to write a new chapter in his career, the ICC World Cup 2015 is the new big challenge for him. All of us know that he has done it before. All of us want to believe he will do it again. At the end of the day, he is nothing if not the Most Successful Doer.

He is MSD.

MSD: FACTS OF FIGURES

Full name:	Mahendra Singh Dhoni. Also known as Mahi
Date of bith:	7 July 1981
Place of birth:	Ranchi, Bihar (now Jharkhand)
Major teams:	India, Asia XI, Bihar, Chennai Super Kings, Jharkhand
Playing role:	Wicketkeeper–batsman
Batting style:	Right-hand bat
Bowling style:	Right-arm medium fast
Fielding position:	Wicketkeeper

BATTING AND FIELDING AVERAGES

	Mat	Inns	NO	Runs	HS	Ave	BF	SR	100	50	4s	6s	Ct	St
Tests	89	142	15	4841	224	38.11	8187	59.13	6	33	539	78	248	37
ODIs	250	219	64	8192	183*	52.85	9175	89.28	9	56	637	177	227	85
T20Is	50	45	20	849	48*	33.96	730	116.30	0	0	57	24	25	11
First–class	130	208	18	7003	224	36.85			9	47			356	56
List A	307	272	75	10195	183*	51.75			15	67			297	100
Twenty20	191	172	65	4035	73*	37.71	2954	136.59	0	16	286	167	90	42

(Updated on 28th October, 2014. Source: www.ESPNcricinfo.com)

ACKNOWLEDGEMENTS

Before I mention the names of those who made *MSD: The Man, the Leader* possible, let me share a small story. Way back in 2004, after I had finished my fourth biography,I had taken a firm decision which had been partly facilitated by the need to finish all of them within one year. How and why I did that, I still cannot explain. But the fact is, I finished them and one new title hit the bookstores after every three months. Extremely tired because of the additional pressure of a full-time job, I refused one big project along similar lines which fell on my lap and promised to myself that I will write another biography only if the subject was irresistible.

Years later, I finally realized that MS Dhoni was that subject. For, here was a man who had challenged his surroundings, grown up amidst adversities and eventually become a rock star of Indian cricket. The idea was to write a jargon-free book that reached out to the average cricket fan as well as those who may not follow the game on a day-to-day basis but want to read the ultimate story of inspiration in Indian cricket.

Many individuals contributed to make this book happen.

Anupam Sheshank, Editor and Publisher, *The Pioneer* (Jharkhand edition) and childhood friend who offered any assistance I needed.

Sambit Bal, Editor in-chief, ESPNcricinfo, with whom I worked for the first time way back in 1992. He permitted the usage of ESPNcricinfo's content, which played a very important role in giving the section on Dhoni's cricketing career the sort of shape it required.

Chandrajit Mukherjee, a Ranchi-based lawyer and journalist who served as the researcher and assisted me with exemplary cooperation and hard work during the Ranchi and Kharagpur phases.

Shubham Mukherjee, the National Business Editor of *The Times of India*. When I needed the presence of corporate leaders in the book, I reached out for him. He helped because he had no choice, having been one year junior to me in school.

Dibakar Ghosh in Rupa for suffering my countless delays with less anger and impatience than I thought was possible. Apart from that, Dibakar's editorial inputs were immensely valuable.

Ratan Lal of *The Pioneer* supplied all the photographs from Ranchi.

Alok Sinha, Sports Editor and Partha Bhaduri, Assistant Editor (Sports) of *The Times of India* (Delhi) extended their support.

Michael Joseph, my former TOI (Pune) colleague put me through to Chandu Borde and Dhanraj Pillay.

How my wife Medha endured my frequent disappearances while being at home is a mystery for me.

Sandipan Deb, a friend first and a professional senior later, for his support, patience and encouragement. For the last twenty plus years, he has always been one telephone call away.

My uncle, who suddenly passed away days after this manuscript was completed. If there was one person who wanted to read this book, it was him.

Finally, Burp and Jack, my two lovely kids. Their endearing innocence teaches me a thing or two about life every day.